NCAA
MARCH MADNESS
SOUTH REGIONAL CHAMPION
CHAMPIONSHIPS
FINAL FOUR
2026 SOUTH REGIONAL CHAMPS
UTH REGIONAL CHAMPS
2026 SOUTH REGIONAL CHAM
AL CHAMPS
I0762409

FLYIN' HIGH AGAIN

CELEBRATING THE FIGHTING ILLINI'S MAGICAL MARCH TO THE FINAL FOUR

The News-Gazette®

The News-Gazette®

Bob Asmussen
Matt Daniels
Jeff D'Alessio
Jim Dey
Niko Dugan
Joel Leizer
Rob Le Cates
Alex Mazur
Zach Piatt
Scott Richey
Jim Rossow
Robin Scholz
Loren Tate
Luke Taylor
Joe Vozzelli
Jana Wiersema
Joey Wright

news-gazette.com

Book design by Josh Crutchmer

The publisher would like to thank Bret Kroencke, Matt Ashmore and Tim Young for all of their tremendous work. Dedicated to Richie Bristow — a true Fighting Illini fan.

ISBN: 978-1-957005-45-4

Printed in the United States of America

CONTENTS

Foreword	**By Loren Tate**	4
Season Opener	**Illini 113, Jackson State 55**	8
Regular Season	**Illini 81, Texas Tech 77**	14
Regular Season	**UConn 74, Illini 61**	20
Regular Season	**Illini 75, Tennessee 62**	22
Regular Season	**Illini 88, Ohio State 80**	26
Regular Season	**Illini 91, Missouri 48**	30
Illini Feature	**Tomislav Ivisic**	34
Regular Season	**Illini 75, Iowa 69**	38
Regular Season	**Illini 88, Purdue 82**	42
Illini Feature	**Keaton Wagler**	46
Regular Season	**Illini 78, Nebraska 69**	56
Regular Season	**Michigan State 85, Illini 82 (OT)**	60
Regular Season	**Illini 71, Indiana 51**	62
Regular Season	**Michigan 84, Illini 70**	66
Regular Season	**Illini 84, Oregon 50**	68
Illini Feature	**Kylan Boswell**	74
Big Ten Tournament	**Wisconsin 91, Illini 88 (OT)**	82
Illini Feature	**David Mirkovic**	84
NCAA First Round	**Illini 105, Penn 70**	88
Illini Feature	**Andrej Stojakovic**	92
NCAA Round of 32	**Illini 76, VCU 55**	98
NCAA Sweet 16	**Illini 65, Houston 55**	104
NCAA Elite 8	**Illini 71, Iowa 58**	110
Illini Feature	**Brad Underwood**	120
Final Four	**UConn 71, Illini 62**	134
Season Recap	**Bright Future Starts Now**	138

FOREWORD

A historic run for the Illini

By LOREN TATE

IN REALITY, SUPERSTARS Ayo Dosunmu, Kofi Cockburn and Terrence Shannon Jr. got it started.

They never reached the NCAA Final Four but they lifted the Illini to basketball's forefront, turning the university into a prime landing spot for not only in-state athletes but international talent as well.

As it turns out, Greece-born Andrej Stojankovic, Montenegro's David Mirkovic and Croatia's 7-foot twins Tomislav and Zvonimir Ivisic not only spark this year's Final Four bid but could provide the nucleus around which to build next season.

Coach Brad Underwood may have difficulty replacing guards like senior Kylan Boswell and likely NBA-bound Keaton Wagler, but that's a concern for another day. The current run found Illinois in the Final Four for just the third time in 74 years — including my 61 years on the beat at *The News-Gazette* and on WDWS.

In 1989, it was Lou Henson's Flyin' Illini who used their unrivaled athleticism to reach Seattle. Along the way, they won over fans and even Dick Vitale, who gave Kenny Battle, Nick Anderson, Kendall Gill, Stephen Bardo, Lowell Hamilton and Co. their nickname.

In 2005, it was Bruce Weber's rock stars who started 29-0 and remained No. 1 in the nation in reaching the program's first championship game — thousands of fans following Dee, Deron and Co. to St. Louis.

In both magical seasons, the quest fell just short.

Illinois is tops among teams that have never won the championship. For all concerned, it was the chance of a lifetime. It slipped away on the night of April 4, with Connecticut staving off a second-half comeback attempt by the Illini to earn a 71-62 win in a national semifinal game.

A national championship will have to wait again for Illinois.

Yet the memories of what the 2025-26 Illini accomplished will live on. In these pages. And in the minds of the thousands of Illini fans who descended upon Indianapolis at the Final Four, not to mention the hundreds of thousands watching across the country and world.

What a ride it was.

Illinois coach Brad Underwood celebrates while cutting down the nets after the Illini's Elite 8 win over Iowa. (Moises Ramos Marin/The News-Gazette)

MARCH
MADNESS

Fans listen to AD Josh Whitman at a sendoff in Champaign as the Illini head to the Final Four. (Robin Scholz/The News-Gazette)

SREĆNO!
FINAL FOUR
Illinois
MIKE WILLIAMS

SEASON OPENER

ILLINI 113, JACKSON STATE 55

November 3, 2025

Playing hard, having fun

Mirkovic heeds coach's instructions, sets tone for Illini in season-opening rout

By SCOTT RICHEY
srichey@news-gazette.com

CHAMPAIGN — Brad Underwood writes the same four words on the whiteboard in the Illinois men's basketball locker room before every game.

Play hard.

Have fun.

Two phrases that just as easily describe the way David Mirkovic approaches the game. The Illini freshman forward does both — in equal measure — and, on occasion, perhaps too much.

Mirkovic flashed his dynamic skill set again in Illinois' season opener against Jackson State on Monday night at State Farm Center. His 19 points, 14 rebounds and four assists during the Illini's 113-55 victory in front of 14,511 fans at State Farm Center were examples of the multiple ways he can affect winning.

Exactly what Underwood wants from the 19-year-old Montenegrin.

What Underwood could use less of is the nearly full-court, underhanded sling of a pass Mirkovic threw late in the first half against the Tigers.

Did it eventually lead to a Jason Jakstys dunk? Yes. Did it almost hit the scoreboard in the process before Jake Davis could get a hand on it? Also yes.

"Coaches were a little bit angry about that pass," Mirkovic said after Monday's blowout win.

"You probably won't see it again," veteran forward Ben Humrichous added. "I hope not."

"Yeah," Mirkovic chimed in before reversing course to leave the door open. "Maybe, if there is a situation, but I will try not to do it."

Underwood said he loves Mirkovic's passion for the game, if not all the decisions he's made with the ball in his hands.

"That's what this should be about is the understanding of having fun playing the game," Underwood said. "He has just tremendous joy for the game. Now, I've got to get him to have fun and not be sloppy. The underhand pass that almost hit the scoreboard is probably not working too well in league play. Those are things that are enjoyable to him. We have to get them a little less enjoyable."

Mirkovic has made quite the impression during his short time so far in Champaign. That includes his effort on the practice court at Ubben Basketball Complex and the way he's performed in Illinois' exhibition game against Illinois State, its scrimmage against reigning NCAA champions Florida and in the season opener against Jackson State.

Mirkovic flirted with a triple-double against the Redbirds. Underwood called him the best player on the court in the second half against the Gators. And he had a double-double locked up before halftime Monday night, making him the first Illinois freshman with a double-double in his debut since Kofi Cockburn put up 11 points and 10 rebounds against Nicholls State nearly six years ago to the day.

"I remember when David came in in the summer. I was like, 'Dude, this guy has a motor where he just plays the whole time really, really hard,'" Humrichous said. "Even through practice, David's been one of those guys that's handled adversity really well. He's

Illinois' David Mirkovic passes the ball as Jackson State's Deyan Kolev guards during the first half. (Associated Press)

SWAC
JACKSON
9
STATE
ELITE

handled Coach Underwood's coaching really well. And he really dived into our process. What he worries about is winning, and he makes some really fun plays in the process.

"He can rebound, and he plays really hard. ... You saw with his touch around the rim with his ability to finish through physicality. A really skilled dude who just plays incredibly hard, and you guys are seeing the fruits of it."

Illinois might have only scratched the surface of Mirkovic's ability. Untethering him from the post, where he spent most of his time the past couple seasons with SC Derby in the Adriatic League, has unlocked the 6-foot-9, 250-pound forward's versatile skill set.

The Illini pursued Mirkovic on the recruiting trail because he was different than returning big man Tomislav Ivisic, and how they'll use the Mirkovic will likely continue to evolve.

"There will be some times he's going to play the point," Underwood said. "We're just going to give him the ball because he's that kind of decision-maker and that type of handler. ... We've seen him shoot it, drive it, pass it, play make. I think those are all the things that good players do.

"It's just putting him in positions to be successful, and the one thing he's proven to us is he can do that. He's still learning. It's going to be harder — maybe — but he's got a unique IQ, he's very cerebral, he's a great problem solver and he's a great teammate."

Jackson State's Deyan Kolev (9) and Tamarion Hoover battle for a rebound with Illinois' Ben Humrichous. (Associated Press)

HUMRICHOUS
3
SWAC
JACKSON
0

The Illini's dance team performs at State Farm Center during the game against Jackson State. (Associated Press)

REGULAR SEASON

ILLINI 81, TEXAS TECH 77

November 11, 2025

'It's why he came here'

Transfer Stojakovic proves his worth with game-high 23 points in early-season test

By **SCOTT RICHEY**
srichey@news-gazette.com

CHAMPAIGN — Kylan Boswell described the way he approached recruiting Andrej Stojakovic to Illinois this past spring as harassment.

Calls. Texts.

Anything to convince Stojakovic that his next stop should be Champaign.

"That's not a joke," Boswell said. "Immediately I was calling this dude. I was probably bugging this kid like, 'Why is he still texting me?' When I found out that we were interested in him, I immediately texted him. He was one of my favorite players I was watching throughout the (offseason) of who we wanted.

"I'm really excited he got here. Big shoutout to me for doing that — 100 percent."

Brad Underwood was willing to let Boswell take the credit for Stojakovic's successful transfer recruitment. An easy stance to take after the 6-foot-7, 215-pound guard just put together his best performance in an Illinois men's basketball uniform on Tuesday night at State Farm Center in a Top 25 matchup against Texas Tech.

Not that there were many to choose from.

Stojakovic missed seven weeks with a knee sprain this fall and was in street clothes when Illinois opened the season Nov. 3 against Jackson State. The California transfer made his debut last Friday against Florida Gulf Coast in an uneven performance where it was clear he had, in fact, missed seven weeks and was making his Illini debut.

What Stojakovic accomplished Tuesday night for No. 14 Illinois in its 81-77 win against No. 11 Texas Tech before a sellout crowd of 15,544 fans at State Farm Center was the exact opposite. He found his rhythm early against the Red Raiders — not missing a shot in the first half — and finished with a team-high 23 points on 11 of 16 shooting to go with three rebounds, three steals and two blocks for the Illini (3-0).

"He's scored a lot of points," Texas Tech coach Grant McCasland said of Stojakovic. "It's not like he doesn't know how to score. That's not the issue. The angles at which we gave him baskets early to gain his confidence is what I think I look back and go, 'Man, that's a major problem.' Honestly, if he's earning a bunch of twos and we make it difficult on him, then it's OK. But when you leave your feet and give up angles and you give him and-ones at the basket, that's a problem.

"He is a tough cover when he gains confidence like that. Just not physical enough at the point of attack."

Texas Tech (2-1) let Stojakovic get comfortable. Big mistake. It let the former McDonald's All-American settle into a place where he could show exactly why he was a priority in the portal and why Underwood was eager to pair him with Boswell in the Illinois backcourt.

"We were very specific in what we were looking for with him," Underwood said. "We had some other guys we chose to let go of and not keep recruiting. It's nice to see that in a really small sample size kind of work out. We'll see as the season goes. ... It's unfortunate, the injury, but he's done everything we've asked for. We'll see how that keeps materializing.

Illinois guard Andrej Stojakovic hustles for the ball against Texas Tech forward JT Toppin. (Robin Scholz/The News-Gazette)

"I think it's a credit to him. He's missed seven weeks. You have a certain expectation level because he's a junior, he's been around. He knows what high-level games look like. He knows what really good players look like being in the ACC. Very, very pleased and probably surprised with the connectivity."

Stojakovic's ability to find his place in Illinois' rotation despite missing nearly two months is tied to his top recruiter. He became close with Boswell when he arrived in Champaign in June. Close enough that Stojakovic invited Boswell home to Greece in the break between the end of summer workouts and the start of the new school year.

"I guess I'm glad he harassed me," Stojakovic quipped. "Having that relationship with Kylan as soon as I got in the portal, by the time I moved in in the summer, we were very close. We went to Greece together. I went to go see my family. We trained. He met all my people, and we got very close. It's been great so far. A very productive summer. The injuries are what they are, but I feel very grateful for my decision."

Stojakovic's knee injury is far from the only issue keeping Illinois away from full health early in the season. Ty Rodgers is out indefinitely following offseason knee surgery. Brandon Lee (ankle) and Mihailo Petrovic (hamstring) have yet to make their Illini debuts, and Tomislav Ivisic (knee) has already been ruled out for a third straight game when Colgate (1-2) visits for an 8 p.m. tip on Friday at State Farm Center.

Those injuries have kept Illinois from reaching its full potential as a team. Seven weeks sidelined did the same for Stojakovic. Or at least delayed it. Tuesday night's performance against Texas Tech looked an awful lot like what Underwood envisioned it could be — particularly on the defensive end of the court.

That's where the Illinois coach saw the biggest area of growth for Stojakovic. Three steals and two blocked shots against the Red Raiders, including a block on Christian Anderson's potential game-tying three-pointer with 9 seconds to play and Illinois clinging to an 80-77 lead, was some of that defensive potential realized.

"He's got great size," Underwood said, detailing Stojakovic's strengths as a defender. "He's got great feet. He's freakishly athletic. I think we'll see that as we continue to see him get into shape. ... The sad thing for me is that I didn't get to demand, for seven weeks, that he guard at a very high level. My whole premise going into the fall was to make him an elite, elite wing defender and hold him to that. He doesn't need to score big every single night for us to win — be a great offensive player — but he does have to guard."

Stojakovic did both Tuesday against Texas Tech, helping deliver Illinois a key ranked win. Exactly what Boswell, Underwood and the Illini were hoping when they recruited him to Champaign.

"Just instant offense for us," Boswell said. "Defensively, the game-winning stop. It's why he came here."

Ben Humrichous snags a rebound in front of Texas Tech's JT Toppin. (Robin Scholz/The News-Gazette)

ILLINOIS

Coach Brad Underwood sees the Orange Krush fans holding up a picture of Underwood and his team during a win over Texas Tech. (Robin Scholz/The News-Gazette)

REGULAR SEASON
UCONN 74, ILLINI 61

November 28, 2025

Searching for toughness, passion

Illini find their best in spurts but ultimately fall to perennial power UConn

By SCOTT RICHEY
srichey@news-gazette.com

NEW YORK — The final fan showed on the Madison Square Garden videoboard ahead of tipoff in Illinois's game against Connecticut was a young Huskies fan holding a sign that let everyone know it was her first game at "Storrs South."

That's the environment the Illini walked into Friday afternoon.

The crowd of 16,154 at the Garden skewed heavily in UConn's favor. The chants of "I-L-L ... I-N-I" got drowned out by the Huskies faithful. Another wrinkle to the not-exactly-neutral site matchup that was challenging enough already against the No. 5 team in the country.

A game like that requires a certain mindset. A different kind of intensity.

Illinois found that level of play only in fits and starts Friday at MSG. An infrequency that turned out to be problematic in a 74-61 loss.

"We need to grit and grind and get grimy in practice," Illinois coach Brad Underwood said. "We had one day this week that we did a drill where I can usually find out who the quitters are because winning is so hard.

"Winning is really, really hard at this level. You're playing a top-five team — basically in front of all their fans — and you have to find a way to win. It's the little things. It's not whether you score a basket. When it's really hard, who goes to make a play? We're not quite there yet."

Getting there? The next week will show if Illinois can find the toughness Underwood is seeking.

The Illini (6-2) don't play again until their Dec. 6 date with Tennessee in Nashville, Tenn. Another not-really-neutral site showdown with the Vols playing less than three hours away from home and Illinois making twice as long a trip.

That week in between games will give Underwood the chance to put his team through the practice wringer. Something he hasn't been able to do in the last couple months, as multiple injuries kept the full team from getting on the court at Ubben Basketball Complex together.

"Just practice," Underwood said was all he wanted. "Make it hard. Stress them. Put demands on them and expectations. Get them tired. Get them mentally tired and pushing them to execute and pushing them to defend. Not making the same mistakes over and over.

"There's accountability to that. I'm putting guys on the court who have not been held accountable through practice because we're playing so many games. We're just trying to play guys into shape. That's been the frustrating thing as a coach."

Lacking the toughness Underwood desires showed up Friday against UConn (6-1). In the Illini's inability to finish at the rim, making just 9 of 22 layups. In the Huskies' edge in the rebounding battle. In shooting just three first-half free throws when shots weren't falling and that could have been a spark to reignite the offense.

Where it began, though, was on the defensive end. UConn's guards got to their spots with little trouble and got shots to fall. Scouting report mistakes left Huskies forward Alex Karaban — a 38 percent career three-point shooter knocking down 50 percent this season — open beyond the arc.

Illinois guard Keaton Wagler fights for a loose ball with UConn guard Malachi Smith, right, and Solo Ball during the second half. (Associated Press)

13

REGULAR SEASON

ILLINI 75, TENNESSEE 62

December 6, 2025

Illini find their difference maker

Wagler thriving under bright lights, biggest stages

By SCOTT RICHEY
srichey@news-gazette.com

NASHVILLE — Keaton Wagler was the last Illinois men's basketball player to make his way through the gauntlet of fans between the court at Bridgestone Arena and the tunnel back to the locker room.

That's what happens when you play a pivotal role in a showdown between Top 25 teams. Postgame media obligations have to be handled even before the press conference begins.

So while the rest of Wagler's teammates had already soaked in the adulation of the Illinois fans that got floor seats Saturday night and those that could get to the front row of the stands to deliver as many high-fives as possible, the freshman guard got that experience to himself.

One young Illinois fan caught Wagler's attention and went home with an autograph from the Shawnee, Kan., native. If there was one autograph to get, that was it, after Wagler finished with 16 points, eight rebounds and five assists in No. 14 Illinois' 75-62 victory against No. 13 Tennessee in front of 16,157 fans.

Another big stage. Another standout performance.

"He can do a little bit of everything," Illinois starting center Tomislav Ivisic said of Wagler. "Great teammate. Great guy. I've seen it from the first day, so I can't say I'm impressed. I know what he's capable of."

Wagler's production in Illinois' big games has been a bit of a mixed bag. That's not all that unexpected given he has just a month of college basketball under his belt. But he's received plenty of reps between the Illini's October scrimmage against Florida and their November games against Texas Tech, Alabama and Connecticut.

Wagler impressed Texas Tech coach Grant McCasland after putting up 11 points and seven rebounds in the Illini's early November victory against the Red Raiders at State Farm Center. Duplicating that against the Crimson Tide and Huskies proved more difficult.

Saturday was his best yet. Wagler scored eight of Illinois' first 14 points to start the second half and delivered a momentum-shifting moment with a three-pointer with just less than eight minutes to play as the answer to a Nate Ament dunk for the Vols.

"I think it got me a lot more comfortable playing these big-time games with more physicality and just better overall players and teams," Wagler said about facing three ranked teams last month. "It's going out there being confident in my game and just try to make plays."

Mission accomplished on the playmaking front.

Wagler created for himself and his teammates, and his five assists were paired with zero turnovers. That impressed Brad Underwood as much — if not more — than the 16 points he scored.

"That's almost every single day," the Illinois coach said. "He just takes care of the ball and is a very mature decision-maker. That's usually not the case for a freshman."

Wagler's game-high 16 points — honors he shared with Ivisic — came on the strength of making four three-pointers.

That's a new career-high for the Illinois freshman. The same was true of his 11

Keaton Wagler shoots the ball past Tennessee guard Ja'Kobi Gillespie during the first half. (Associated Press)

Illinois
23
TENNESSEE
0
VOLUNTEERS

attempts, which was nearly double his next highest total this season.

"I just let the game come to me," Wagler said. "I had a lot of open shots and also had some late shot-clock shots that came to me. I knew when I had a mismatch I could get to my move and get to my three. A lot of them felt really good. Some of them didn't fall, but some did. It wasn't a really big emphasis, but I let the ball come to me."

That approach is why plenty about what Wagler has accomplished in the first month of the season is atypical for a freshman. Part of that stems from his high basketball IQ and understanding of what's expected of him on the court in Illinois' system. Underwood also credits Kylan Boswell's influence.

"Keaton just plays," Underwood added. "The environment doesn't bother him. Maybe a little bit of the physicality. It's just a matter of him getting comfortable. We didn't talk one second about shooting threes, but that's what he does. We've needed him to be more aggressive and more assertive."

Illinois guard Andrej Stojakovic shoots the ball past Tennessee forward J.P. Estrella, right, during the second half. (Associated Press)

ABRAM
77

REGULAR SEASON
ILLINI 88, OHIO STATE 80

December 9, 2025

Major road test passed

Freshmen propel Illini to Big Ten road win after withstanding physical Ohio State

By **SCOTT RICHEY**
srichey@news-gazette.com

COLUMBUS, Ohio — The final minute of Tuesday night's game at Value City Arena was the perfect illustration of the depth that could make Illinois men's basketball a Big Ten title contender this season.

Offensive/defensive substitutions with 7-foot Croatian twins Tomislav and Zvonimir Ivisic featured a clutch three-pointer from the former, where he got a favorable roll after missing his first five three-pointers of the game, and two key defensive stops by the latter. Freshmen Keaton Wagler and David Mirkovic, clearly trusted down the stretch, knocked down six free throws.

Wagler finished with a team-high 23 points, Mirkovic added 22 and No. 13 Illinois topped Ohio State 88-80 in its Big Ten opener in front of a crowd of 9,974 at the Jerome Schottenstein Center.

"It was a good basketball team we were able to fend off," Illinois coach Brad Underwood said. "I'm proud of our guys coming off a very emotional game after a hard week of practice (and beating Tennessee) and having to turn right back around come to Ohio State. ... The first half was just back and forth, everybody making shots. The second half turned into a Big Ten basketball game in terms of the rugged-type play."

Illinois (8-2, 1-0 Big Ten) handled that physicality and, the Illini's balance helped offset a big night from Bruce Thornton. The veteran guard and four-year starter made his first nine shots, including six three-pointers, got to halftime with 24 points and finished with a game-high 34 points for the Buckeyes (7-2, 1-1).

Thornton eventually got some help, which was needed with Illinois slowing him down during the final 20 minutes.

"They changed their defensive coverage, and I trust my teammates to make shots," Thornton said. "I'm going to keep passing it. What I did was OK, but it wasn't good enough to win."

But even with more from John Mobley Jr. and Devin Royal in the second half, Ohio State still couldn't match Illinois' depth.

Andrej Stojakovic got back on track after two uncharacteristically poor performances with 17 points, and Zvonimir Ivisic provided 13 points and eight rebounds off the bench. That effort from the 7-2 backup big man was something the Buckeyes had no answer for with just two points from their reserves. Those veterans provided productive minutes, but it was Illinois' freshmen starters impressing in their first Big Ten game. Mirkovic added nine rebounds to go with his 22 points buoyed by 4 of 5 three-point shooting and making all eight of his free throws.

Wagler's 23 points gave him double-digit production in two straight games after his 16-point effort in Saturday's win against Tennessee. The 6-6 guard made 3 of 5 three-pointers and 8 of 9 free throws.

"He's a good player," Thornton said. "I feel like we let him get in a rhythm. Any good player, when they catch a rhythm, it's hard to stop them. He got a couple wide-open looks for three. ... He was constantly in a rhythm seeing the ball go in."

Wagler played 39 of 40 minutes against Ohio State and didn't come off the court in

Ohio State's Bruce Thornton and Illinois' David Mirkovic fight for the ball during the first half. (Associated Press)

ELITE

the second half.

His first-half performance was key, though, with Stojakovic dealing with some foul trouble and Boswell struggling to get into much of a rhythm offensively. Wagler scored 14 of his team-high 23 points during the first half and had four of his five assists in those 19 minutes.

"I thought I had to be more aggressive on the ball," Wagler said. "I just tried to let the game come to me and not do too much. ... I just tried to keep myself loose, smile out there and have fun playing the game. My whole life I've played in big moments, and I feel like this is just another one of those."

Illinois' Andrej Stojakovic shoots over Ohio State's John Mobley, center, and Bruce Thornton during the second half. (Associated Press)

Safelite

REGULAR SEASON
ILLINI 91, MISSOURI 48

December 22, 2025

'All you have to do is go to the glass'

Illini control the paint and handle Missouri with ease

By SCOTT RICHEY
srichey@news-gazette.com

ST. LOUIS — Efficient, effective offense has rarely been an issue in Brad Underwood's tenure leading a men's college basketball program. Particularly at the high-major level.

Underwood's lone Oklahoma State team finished the 2016-17 season ranked first nationally in adjusted offensive efficiency.

A wicked combination of offensive rebounding and three-point shooting helped the Cowboys overcome a 0-6 start in Big 12 play to reach the NCAA tournament with the high-scoring trio of Jawun Evans, Jeffrey Carroll and Phil Forte bolstered by Mitchell Solomon's ability to corral more than his share of offensive rebounds.

Not all of Underwood's teams at Illinois have produced at that level.

But they're becoming more commonplace. The 2020-21 team that had the best record in the Big Ten and earned a No. 1 seed in the NCAA tournament had a top 10 offense behind Ayo Dosunmu and Kofi Cockburn. The 2023-24 team that reached the Elite Eight was ranked No. 1 nationally in adjusted offensive efficiency before its loss to Connecticut.

Last year's team finished in the top 15. This year's team trails only Alabama after Monday night's 91-48 blowout win against Missouri to secure a third straight Braggin' Rights victory. A 43-point rout, the largest in series history against the Tigers, built on that same combination of offensive rebounding and three-point shooting.

Illinois (9-3) turned 15 offensive rebounds into 29 second-chance points, failing to convert on just three of those opportunities. The Illini also made 15 of 33 three-pointers, with only the season opener against Jackson State yielding more makes (17) at a higher percentage (46 percent) this season beyond the arc.

"The thing that helps us more than anything is offensive rebounding," Underwood said. "That's all I harp on. I think if you ask every player the thing I talk about the most, and it's offensive rebounding. We work on it every single day getting guys to create habits. That leads to your efficiency. That leads to fouls being drawn. That leads to unguarded threes.

"Those are the baskets you don't have to grind and earn, and all you have to do is go to the glass. Our efficiency, our abilities on that end, are really predicated on being able to (offensive rebound) at a high level."

Illinois turned four offensive rebounds into made three-pointers during the first half on Monday night. That included three in a row — makes from deep by Keaton Wagler, Ben Humrichous and Jake Davis — that pushed the Illini's lead to double figures. An advantage that only grew the rest of the game.

"When everyone crashes the glass, teams get worn out from that and they don't really want to box out every time," Wagler said. "We know if we all go, we're going to get the ball. That's easy points. Second-chance points are really big in these types of games. That's what got our offense going."

Missouri couldn't keep Illinois off the boards. Wagler and Zvonimir Ivisic hauled in four offensive rebounds apiece. Six other Illini all pulled down one each.

"Early on I though it was nip tuck, but

Illini players celebrate with the Braggin' Rights trophy after a blowout win over Missouri in St. Louis (Knox Mynatt/The News-Gazette)

Illinois
2
13

ultimately that run, giving up the second-chance points we gave up, they executed on every single one of them," Missouri coach Dennis Gates said. "That's what hurt. That's what ignited their run. They were able to get their hands on a lot of those rebounds. Once they secured it, they ended up executing. It was just make after make on those second chances."

Illinois' 15 offensive rebounds against Missouri were the team's most this season since grabbing 19 against Colgate on Nov. 14. The Illini set the bar even higher in that same season opener on Nov. 3 against Jackson State with 21 offensive rebounds.

The effort show to crash the offensive glass Monday night with Braggin' Rights on the line is what Underwood didn't see enough of from his team in the first two Big Ten games of the season or at other points throughout the first two months of the season.

It's why Underwood made it even more of a point of emphasis in every practice between losing at home to Nebraska on Dec. 13 and getting back on the court Monday against Missouri.

"We spent nine days on it," Underwood said. "Every coach was dialed in. A point of emphasis in every aspect of our practice was going to the glass. Not laying on backs. Not accepting a blockout. David (Mirkovic) got one early in the game, a foul called, because he laid on a back and pushed. That's what we're trying to get away from. You've got to make the second and third effort. We've got to continually work on this and get better at it if we want to be the team, offensively, that we think we can be.

"We're emphasizing it. We're demanding it. For us to get where we want to go and be as efficient on the offensive end as I think we can be, that's a big piece of it."

Consider the message received. Illinois showed how effective its offense can be in running up the score against Missouri on Monday night in St. Louis.

"A lot of attention to detail over the week," Illini guard Andrej Stojakovic said. "A lot of preparation. Intense practices, which is what we needed with that many days off in between games. We knew we had to come out with a certain type of energy. We came out with that, and we jumped them."

Illinois' Zvonimir Ivisic knocks away a shot beneath the basket from Missouri's Annor Boateng. (Associated Press)

Illinois
B1G
MIRKOVIC
0

‘Just a force’ at his best

By SCOTT RICHEY
srichey@news-gazette.com

CHAMPAIGN — Brad Underwood expressed zero concerns with Tomislav Ivisic after the 7-foot-1 center went scoreless with just two rebounds and twice as many fouls in Illinois’ win against Penn State in Philadelphia.

The Illini coach might not have put any credence to Ivisic struggling, but it was the third straight Big Ten game the Croatian big man had not played to the expectations his previous efforts had set for his base line performance.

Ivisic had seven points and two rebounds in Illinois’ Big Ten road win at Ohio State. Then three points, five rebounds, two assists and two blocks in the home loss to Nebraska before playing objectively his worst game of the season at the Palestra last weekend.

Thursday night was different. Ivisic put up 14 points and four rebounds — scoring in multiple ways — to help No. 16 Illinois knock off Rutgers 81-55.

“It’s always good to help the team win — especially after a couple bad games from my end,” Ivisic said.

Underwood never categorized Ivisic’s other performances in Big Ten play that way. At least not when asked, as he was after the win against Penn State and again earlier this week before the Rutgers game.

The only ask Underwood is making of Ivisic is to provide more as a rebounder.

“Everyone has a bad game or sees a coverage or sees something that doesn’t allow you to maybe have your best night,” Underwood said. “He got a couple baskets cutting (against Rutgers). He got a three here or there. He got a post up. He got a wide array of what his capabilities are.

“It was just a matter of taking advantage of the coverage. We’re not a big set team. We’re just going to play on the coverages and the reads, and I think the thing he did the best was cut and move.”

Ivisic has been playing catch up most of this season. He was sidelined for a significant portion of Illinois’ preseason practices after an illness dictated a tonsillectomy. A knee injury following the season opener cost him three games in November and provided another setback to his efforts in regaining the level of conditioning he developed during intense summer workouts with strength and conditioning coach Adam Fletcher.

“I missed a lot of time in the beginning of practice,” Ivisic said. “The team was already in their own track, and I was kind of chasing after them, following after them. I feel like I came back to good shape pretty quick. I’m just trying to do my part and help the team win, and, also for myself, be the best I can and play hard. Be better.”

Missed time — both before the season and again in November — also meant having to find how he fit with a new-look Illinois team on the court after they’d developed something of a rhythm without him. Roster retention might have been higher for the Illini ahead of this season compared to the offseason prior, but this year’s team has different strengths.

“My role is different,” Ivisic said. “Definitely being more of a spacer. We’ve got great guards this year. It’s being a great

teammate, setting screens and getting rebounds. Trying to help the team win no matter what it takes."

Ivisic's contributions in Thursday's win against Rutgers stood out to his teammates. It was closer to what Jake Davis saw from the 7-footer last season. Closer to what helped draw Andrej Stojakovic to Champaign.

"I think Tomi's just a force," Davis said. "When he's playing well, he's one of the best centers in college basketball."

"Tomi is a big reason of why I decided to come here — a big who can space the floor," Stojakovic added. "So talented offensively, but just a beast on the defensive side when we're in drop coverage. When he gets going, he's very important for us."

Tomislav Ivisic (left) and Zvonimir Ivisic leave the court following a win over Northwestern . (Robin Scholz/The News-Gazette)

REGULAR SEASON
ILLINI 75, IOWA 69

January 11, 2026

Boswell: 'I'm a pest'

Senior puts Iowa star Stirtz in a vise in front of a hostile road crowd

By SCOTT RICHEY
srichey@news-gazette.com

IOWA CITY, Iowa — Kylan Boswell's preparation for Sunday's game at No. 19 Iowa included plenty of film review on Bennett Stirtz.

Stirtz is one of the top guards in the Big Ten. An honorable mention All-American a year ago at Drake, the 6-foot-4, 190-pound Stirtz is finding similar levels of success after following coach Ben McCollum across the state of Iowa to play for the Hawkeyes.

Boswell drew the primary defensive assignment on Stirtz. The veteran Illinois guard was going to make sure he was prepared, armed with a mentality that he was going to become one of the few defenders to shut Stirtz down considering Stirtz came into Sunday's showdown with No. 16 Illinois averaging 18.0 points.

Preparation that included plenty of emphasis on that matchup from Brad Underwood and his Illinois coaching staff.

"They were on my tail all week," Boswell said. "You know how Coach Brad can be talking smack to me, hyping me up."

Boswell followed through on his pregame intentions. The 6-2, 215-pound senior wanted to set the tone for Sunday's game — for the trouble Stirtz would face — from the opening tip. An aggressive tact that succeeded.

Boswell locked up Stirtz, fed off his defensive energy on the offensive end and helped Illinois fend off a late Iowa rally for a 75-69 victory in front of 13,559 fans at Carver-Hawkeye Arena. A fourth Big Ten win in five games and third straight away from State Farm Center for the Illini (13-3, 4-1 Big Ten).

"I didn't want him to get comfortable," Boswell said of Stirtz, who scored 12 points for the Hawkeyes but needed 17 shots to get there. "I tried to set the tone with my aggressiveness and let him know I was here. ... There were times in the pick-and-roll, if he was too lackadaisical with the ball, I was trying to pressure him and make things tough for him.

"One of the biggest things is I'm a pest. I don't really get tired very often defensively. That was probably my biggest key."

Stirtz felt that pressure. From Boswell. From Andrej Stojakovic and Keaton Wagler. From anyone else who wound up switched on to him during the course of the game.

"They were throwing everyone at me," Stirtz said. "They tried to change it up, and it worked. They made us uncomfortable. Credit to them."

Boswell's lockdown effort on Stirtz was far from the first time the Illinois guard has been asked to come through in a high-profile matchup during his two seasons with the Illini. It doesn't even have to be another guard. Boswell's defense on Texas Tech forward JT Toppin changed the dynamic of that Nov. 11 game in Champaign that marked Illinois' first victory this season against a ranked opponent.

"He finds a way to annoy," Underwood said of Boswell. "He's strong. He picks your pocket. He fights over screens. It wasn't just him, but it was him setting the tone. He's just a veteran. He's got tremendous skills and can do that to a lot of people."

Underwood made a point to note how Boswell starts to thrive offensively when he's dialed in defensively. That was the

Illinois guard Kylan Boswell defends Iowa's Bennett Stirtz in the first half. (Associated Press)

B1G
B1G
FIGHTING
4
ILLINI

case Sunday against Iowa, with Boswell consistently attacking the basket and finishing at the rim to score 17 points on 7 of 13 shooting.

A team-high three steals helped fuel those offensive efforts. Steals that came with Boswell, according to Stirtz, picking and choosing his spots to really attack on defense.

"It drives me nuts because I'd like to see it all the time," Underwood quipped. "It's the one thing Kylan has the ability to do is really sit down and guard — especially in moments where he feels a little bit like his opponent's fatigued or tired. Then he pushes the go button. Great athlete. Great conditioned athlete, and he just has that knack.

"I've learned to trust him and then get frustrated when it doesn't work, but it's what he does at a very, very high level. He's right most of the time."

Boswell's dual effect on Stirtz on Sunda included getting the Iowa guard in foul trouble. Stirtz was whistled for his fourth foul with 11 minutes, 36 minutes remaining in the second half and spent the next seven minutes on the bench.

Iowa (12-4, 2-3) rallied without its scoring leader on the court, but Illinois found a way to fend off that charge. Boswell scoring nine points in that stretch, with Keaton Wagler responsible for the other 11, certainly helped.

"We just had to adjust," said Illinois guard Andrej Stojakovic, who also scored 17 points in the road win. "They went on a run. The ball moved a lot more when Stirtz was out of the game — a lot more back cuts that we made some mistakes on. It's their home court in Big Ten play. We knew they were going to go on a run. We just had to stay poised at the end of the game and make plays."

Andrej Stojakovic drives to the basket past Iowa forward Cooper Koch during the first half. (Associated Press)

Iowa
8
26
7
ILLINI
FIGHTING
0
ILLINI
13

REGULAR SEASON
ILLINI 88, PURDUE 82

January 24, 2026

Wagler steps up ... again

Unflappable guard leads Illinois to major Big Ten win on the road

By **SCOTT RICHEY**
srichey@news-gazette.com

WEST LAFAYETTE, Ind. —Tomislav Ivisic was the first person to reach Keaton Wagler after the final horn sounded on the No. 11 Illinois men's basketball team's 88-82 upset of No. 4 Purdue on Saturday afternoon at Mackey Arena.

Ivisic landed a flying shoulder block before wrapping up Wagler in a bear hug. Then came a low five into a chest bump from Brandon Lee before Wagler was basically swarmed by his Illinois teammates.

Then Wagler had to hit pause on celebrating. A postgame interview on Fox with former Arizona star turned analyst Miles Simon was up first. A quick video hit for Fox's college basketball social media account was filmed next before Wagler ran off Keady Court, up the tunnel and back toward the visiting locker room. Where his teammates were waiting to continue the celebration with water bottles primed to be emptied.

That's what happens when you score more points than any other opposing player in Mackey Arena history.

What happens when you double up your career-high with a 46-point performance. What happens when you lead your team to a significant upset to mark nine straight wins overall and a fifth straight on the road in Big Ten play this season.

"It was crazy," Wagler said of the postgame celebration. "They were all coming up grabbing me, hugging me, saying a bunch of stuff. I walk into the locker room all hype, and they were just spraying water in my face. I couldn't see anything. It was a lot of fun."

Wagler, so stoic on the court, couldn't keep the smile off his face in the moments after Illinois (17-3, 8-1 Big Ten) secured its first win at Mackey Arena since the 2019-20 season. Couldn't keep from letting some emotions out in the locker room either after his performance in front of a sold-out crowd of 14,876 fans.

"He was lit in the locker room," Illinois forward Jake Davis said. "He was yelling a lot — big time."

The complete opposite of the methodical way Wagler — who doubled up as Co-Big Ten Player of the Week and Big Ten Freshman of the Week on Monday — dissected Purdue on national TV on Saturday afternoon. Where his calm, cool and collected on-court persona meant he didn't flinch in arguably the biggest game of the season to date.

Nothing the Boilermakers (17-3, 7-2) tried defensively worked. Switching every screen, leaving big men on the Illinois guard, was a disaster. The 6-foot-6, 185-pound Wagler either beat them off the dribble for a shot at the rim or, more frequently, drilled a stepback jumper from well beyond the three-point line.

Abandoning the switch and sending two defenders to try and keep the ball out of his hands in the finial minutes of a close game was just as ineffective. That's when Wagler found his teammates open on the perimeter, and David Mirkovic, Davis and Ivisic (twice) knocked down clutch three-pointers.

"He just plays," Illinois coach Brad Underwood said about Wagler. "He just hoops. There's nothing that fazes him. He just wants to make the right basketball play. (Saturday) it happened to be scoring it. It's

David Mirkovic celebrates after a second-half basket against Purdue. (Associated Press)

B1G
Illinois
0

just his personality. He's so stoic. He's very non-emotional. He's excited, yes, and his teammates were thrilled, but that's the beauty of Keaton. The more impressive thing is he takes the emotion out of it in a venue with 15,000 people all against him, and he just plays."

Purdue's switching defense created space for Wagler to operate on the perimeter. He beat Boilermakers center Oscar Cluff off the dribble for his first bucket before a cavalcade of three-pointers — nine of them by game's end — that set a single-game program record. Wagler never pressed, and said his teammates understood that it was his night, got him the ball and let him work.

"He just kept going, and he got 46," Mirkovic said. "It's crazy. I don't even have words to describe that. Best performance, for sure, I've ever seen. Just incredible."

"I've been around some guys who can score the ball and put up big nights, but for someone to come into Mackey and put up 46 that's one of the biggest nights I've seen," Davis added. "He's a great player. He's so gifted at everything. He's a great scorer. He's a great passer. One of his most valuable traits is he makes the right decision all the time. He had 46, and toward the end of the game with that much time left he makes the right play."

The way Wagler was able to pick apart the Purdue defense as a facilitator at the end of the game is why the Boilermakers had switched every screen for the majority of the game. They wanted to avoid getting into defensive rotations given how many other shooters were on the court for the Illini, but letting Wagler loose as a scorer in a close game in the final minutes seemed just as untenable.

"What you saw at the end of the game is what we adjusted and did, and you obviously see we're in scramble mode," Purdue coach Matt Painter said. "We wanted to stay out of those rotations and then play him and try to be in gaps. He hit a lot of tough shots over us."

Wagler and Purdue's Braden Smith went shot for shot for part of the second half as Saturday's game came down to the wire. Smith finished with 27 points and 12 assists, but it wasn't enough to offset the best game of Wagler's career that left the reigning Big Ten Player of the Year and All-American guard rather impressed.

"He's probably a lottery pick," Smith said. "I just think he's pretty special, to be honest. We were trying to switch stuff and make them go make one-on-one plays. He hit a lot of tough shots, a lot of high-caliber shots a tough player makes. He played an unbelievable game, and he beat us."

Keaton Wagler drives around Purdue guard Jack Benter. (Associated Press)

Illinois
23
14
13:57
15

An 'untraditional path' for Wagler

By SCOTT RICHEY
srichey@news-gazette.com

CHAMPAIGN — Jennifer Wagler easily recalls a funny moment with her youngest son when he was a toddler.

A moment and conversation that, more than a decade later, is starting to feel just a bit ironic given the basketball path Keaton Wagler has followed.

"He said, 'Is there a job where you can just shoot baskets?'" Jennifer Wagler told The News-Gazette with a smile. "I was like, 'Well, yes, but don't worry about that. You just have fun.'"

Basketball has proven fun for Wagler.

The Shawnee, Kan., native grew up around the game. Both of his parents played at Hutchinson Community College in Kansas in the mid-1990s. His older sister, Brooklyn, played at MidAmerica Nazarene and is now the junior varsity girls' basketball coach at Shawnee Mission Northwest High School in Kansas. Older brother, Landon, is finishing out his collegiate career at MidAmerica Nazarene after stints at Kansas Wesleyan and Hutchinson.

"At a young age, Keaton was watching his older siblings," said Logan Wagler, Keaton's dad. "He seemed locked in. He could not wait for his turn to start playing. Since the moment he could dribble a basketball, he just loved the game and went all-in on it."

That included Wagler winning a state championship at Shawnee Mission Northwest as a junior, when the Cougars went undefeated, and again as a senior. The 6-foot-6 guard parlayed that success into a scholarship at Illinois.

Now, 13 games into his Illini career, it's not a stretch to think that conversation about shooting baskets becoming a job should be revisited.

The 18-year-old Wagler leads No. 20 Illinois (10-3, 1-1 Big Ten) in scoring, assists and steals as conference play resumes in the new year with a 6 p.m. Saturday showdown with Penn State (9-4, 0-2) at the historic Palestra in Philadelphia. The freshman guard is also shooting a team-best 42 percent from three-point range — on nearly five attempts per game — while tied for second on the Illini in rebounding with 7-2 forward Zvonimir Ivisic.

That level of production has made an impression. So has the way the young Illinois guard handled himself on the court during a challenging first two months that featured five games against ranked opponents.

Impressive enough Wagler's name has started popping up on mocks for the 2026 NBA draft. A baker's dozen worth of games that already has him projected as high as the No. 18 overall pick in Bleacher Report Jonathan Wasserman's mock draft.

"Opinions are still being formed on Keaton Wagler, who was off scouts' radar entering the season," Wasserman wrote last month, while giving 2021 News-Gazette All-State Player of the Year Max Christie as a player comp for Wagler. Christie spent one season at Michigan State, was an early second-round pick in the 2022 NBA draft and is now a key part of the Dallas Mavericks rotation after being traded by the Los Angeles Lakers last season in the Luka Doncic deal.

"He has their attention now with 6-6 size, a smooth shooting stroke, nifty ball-

Keaton Wagler poses during the Illini's preseason media day. (Rob LeCates/The News-Gazette)

23

handling skills and a knack for improvising," Wasserman's evaluation of Wagler continued. "Positional size, tight handles, strong shooting indicators and good decision-making suddenly have Wagler in the one-and-done conversation."

That's the kind of out-of-left-field turn of events that can make even a proud pair of parents a little shocked.

Jennifer Wagler used the word "crazy" to describe her youngest son popping up on mock drafts roughly one-third of the way through his freshman year of college basketball. Her husband agreed.

"Absolutely crazy," Logan Wagler added. "We look at it, though, as one step at a time. He's focused on being here, helping this team win. ... It's cool to hear and obviously very exciting for him, but the way our approach has been as a family is one step at a time. Let's just enjoy the moment. Let's stay in the moment. Keep grinding with an every single game matters type of mentality."

'He's fun to coach'

Wagler has made almost every game matter so far this season for Illinois.

He first drew praise from outside Ubben Basketball Complex after putting up 11 points and seven rebounds during the Illini's win against Texas Tech on Nov. 11. Red Raiders coach Grant McCasland was impressed. While there were some tough moments against Alabama and Connecticut in November, Wagler's efforts in December sent his stock skyrocketing.

First came 16 points, eight rebounds and five assists as Illinois took down Tennessee in Nashville, Tenn., on Dec. 6. Then a 23-point effort in his Big Ten debut at Ohio State on Dec. 9, a double-double against Nebraska on Dec. 13, a starring role in his first Braggin' Rights game against Missouri on Dec. 22 and nearly a triple-double against Southern this past Monday.

Five games, four Illinois wins and 18.2 points on 50/50/86 shooting to go with 6.8 assists and 5.2 rebounds per game for the star freshman.

"Good, just good," Illinois coach Brad Underwood said to describe Wagler's play this season. "I'm not going to put an expectation on him. I'm not going to put a ceiling on him. He's not afraid of the moment. He's a really, really good basketball player. When you get really good basketball players, you enjoy them. He's very coachable. He wants to continue to learn and be educated and grow.

"He's fun to coach. I get on him in practice and ride him, and he's stoic. He's got an emotional balance that is very mature, and now I think he's starting to see confidence come from his teammates toward him. He just takes the moment all in stride. His poise is well beyond his years, and it's pretty impressive to see."

'We have a diamond in the rough'

That Wagler has asserted himself in the conversation both as Illinois' best player and a potential one-and-done, first-round pick is quite the surprise. At least to everyone outside his circle.

Illinois was one of just two high-major programs to offer Wagler a scholarship. Murray State, Southern Illinois and Colorado State were also involved late in the process. The Illini got Wagler on campus for an

Wagler shoots after a hard foul by Wisconsin's Andrew Rohde at the State Farm Center in Champaign. (Robin Scholz/The News-Gazette)

ILLINOIS
23

official visit on Sept. 13, 2024, he officially committed five days later and then signed on Nov. 14, 2024.

Wagler jumped from the No. 215 overall prospect in the Class of 2025 to the No. 150 recruit when he committed to Illinois. Perhaps a knee-jerk reaction on the rankings front given his sudden elevation to future Big Ten guard. At one point, in the summer before his senior season at Shawnee Mission Northwest, Wagler's ranking was at No. 298 in his class.

"He didn't play on a high-level circuit," Shawnee Mission Northwest coach David Birch said. "He had an option going into his senior year he could have played EYBL for MOKAN or KC Run GMC on the (Under Armour) circuit. He actually turned them down and chose not to. His reasoning for that is he's just a super loyal guy."

Wagler eschewed a bigger platform on Nike's EYBL circuit or with KC Run GMC to continue playing for VWBA on an independent team. Victor Williams trained Wagler when he was younger, and there was a strong, established relationship.

"He got invites from multiple teams," Logan Wagler said. "He talked to them, was very polite and considered it, but ultimately stuck to his values. He felt that was more important to trust his coach and develop in the right way than go chase the shoe circuit. We're very grateful it worked out, but it was a very untraditional path."

Meanwhile, Birch was spreading the world about Wagler as best he could. That Wagler was 5-8 as a freshman at Shawnee Mission Northwest and still a skinny 6-footer as a sophomore kept him under the radar.

But he kept growing — a lot — while maintaining his skill set. Something Birch had seen previously as an assistant at Blue Valley Northwest (Kan.) when Christian Braun arrived at Kansas before winning the 2022 NCAA title with the Jayhawks and landing with the Denver Nuggets that year as a first-round pick.

"I told everybody," Birch said. "I think a lot of the big schools were concerned with how skinny he was and he'd have trouble adjusting to the physicality of the game. ... Some of it is just the way he looks. It's not necessarily that he's not strong. I don't know if a lot of people saw it like that. I think they saw that and I think they saw he wasn't on a high-level circuit and most people just dubbed him as a mid-major (prospect).

"I talked to (Kansas) a bunch and I said, 'I really think this guy is on that level.' ... At 6-6, it changes everything. He can see everything. He's long. The shot is harder to contest."

Tyler Underwood apparently saw what other coaches on the recruiting trail didn't. The Illinois assistant coach got his first look at Wagler in Chicago at an independent event in the summer of 2024 and liked what he saw enough to make multiple trips to the southwest Kansas City suburbs in late summer and early fall.

Birch said Tyler Underwood was impressed with Wagler's combination of skill and basketball IQ. The latter — the way Wagler made reads on offense and could handle a defensive scouting report — popped the most.

"Tyler came down and watched him a lot in the fall and he had said, 'Hey, man. This guy is skilled. You can see the IQ. I think we

Keaton Wagler passes against Rio Grande Valley's Jaylen Washington. (Robin Scholz/The News-Gazette)

23

have a diamond in the rough here,'" Birch said. "I said, 'I think you do, too. You want me to keep it quiet?' ... Guys that know basketball saw it. Guys that didn't really know what they were looking at really didn't see it."

That Wagler went overlooked and under-recruited didn't escape his notice. It served as motivation.

"Most people thought I might not play as a freshman," he said. "Coming in here, working hard, having a chip on my shoulder, I just like to play as hard as I can knowing I can compete with anyone on the court."

'He just plays his game'

Wagler arrived in Champaign this past summer to zero outside expectations, yet rapidly growing expectations inside the walls of Ubben. Not that his parents would have known their youngest son was turning the heads of his teammates and coaches without hearing from the Illinois staff.

"The coaches were in communication with us throughout the summer," Logan Wagler said. "They were giving us a lot more good feedback than Keaton was. That was kind of comical."

"He would say, 'It's going good,'" Jennifer Wagler added. "I'm like, 'OK, great.'"

Birch had a better idea of the strides Wagler made in June and July in Champaign. He kept in regular contact with Tyler Underwood, who was sending positive reports almost immediately.

"Within a week, they were already texting and saying how good he was looking," Birch said. "I knew that text was coming. I just didn't know it was going to be so early."

Then word on Wagler's potential started making its way outside of the Illinois basketball compound. That Brad Underwood compared him favorably to Kasparas Jakucionis and Will Riley during the Illini's on-campus media day in October was notable. Both were first-round draft picks last summer after a one-and-done season in Champaign, and the Illinois coach said Wagler was the same kind of prospect.

Andrej Stojakovic saw some of that during Illinois' summer workouts. The California transfer said it was hard to miss Wagler holding his own, fitting in and finding ways to get to his spots. When Stojakovic went down with an early fall knee injury, he got a different perspective on his freshman teammate.

Seeing Wagler from the sideline — from a coach's perspective — shed even more light on his ability.

"He's a very simple guy," Stojakovic said. "He doesn't overcomplicate things. He just plays his game. Watching it from the sideline was when I was most impressed. Just watching him and not really playing against him. He plays with such a smooth pace. The physicality doesn't affect him. He's a thin player, but he's so smooth and such a finesse player that he's not really bothered by anything."

Count Birch among those not surprised with how Wagler has played in his first 13 games for Illinois. At least not that it happened. It's only the speed at which Wagler has carved out such a prominent role for the Illini that even Birch didn't expect for his former point guard. Wagler played for Shawnee Mission Northwest as a freshman, teaming up with his older brother, Landon, that year, for a reason. The same reason he started as a sophomore and turned into a star as a junior and senior while winning

Keaton Wagler battles Rutgers guard Jamichael Davis. (Robin Scholz/The News-Gazette)

Illinois
23

a pair of state titles.

"The basketball IQ and the feel is something you can't really teach a guy to do," Birch said. "We try to do a lot of high-level stuff here as far as our scouts — defensive coverages, sets — so that maybe once guys get to college they've seen a lot of that stuff before. He's always had such a good feel for the game."

Shawnee Mission Northwest went 80-16 in four seasons with Wagler on the roster. The Cougars were 25-0 during their unbeaten title run during the 2023-24 season and posted a 22-3 record during the 2024-25 season to repeat as state champions.

"You watch a high school basketball game, you'll rarely watch a tape where a kid will go through an entire game or even an entire week and you feel like he didn't make a wrong read of the defense," Birch said. "That's just something that he does. He's very good at reading what they want to do. He plays at his pace. He's highly skilled. He can shoot. He can dribble the ball. He can pass it. He won't screw up any coverage. I knew he was going to be really good, and Underwood was going to love him.

"I thought he would be good, but to think he was going to be this good, this early, it's not really a surprise to me but the fact it's taken him almost no time to adjust to the speed and the physicality is just even more impressive."

'We never imagined this'

Saturday night's game against Penn State is the first of 19 more guaranteed for Wagler and Illinois this season — 18 more regular-season Big Ten matchups and at least one game in the Big Ten tournament.

It's an opportunity for the Illinois freshman to keep building on the strong foundation he set in his first 13 games. A start to his college career that was as unexpected as it has been celebrated.

"We just wanted him to find his way onto the team, settle in to the routine and requirements around being at the Division I level like this," Logan Wagler said. "For us, we were hoping he could carve out some playing time — a role on this team — and just find a way to help them win. We never imagined this playing out like this.

"It's been really surreal, exciting and also a little bit nerve-wracking at times," Jennifer Wagler added. "For mom, anyway. We understand there's a process. It happened pretty quickly."

Quickly enough that Wagler might find himself facing a stay-or-go situation by season's end. His focus remains squarely on Illinois — on trying to help push the program to its first national championship — and he's supported in that by his family.

But the 2026 NBA draft will continue to loom if Wagler plays as well in his next 19 games as he did in his first 13. That job shooting baskets could come sooner than later.

"He's a smart guy," Birch said. "The family is great. They're not going to make any decisions to leave until they're for sure and until they see it. If he thinks it's in his best interest to come back, he'll probably come back. He's so loyal that he's not going to be out there searching for money or the transfer portal. He's going to stay with guys who believed in him and who have developed him."

Keaton Wagler snags a rebound in front of teammate David Mirkovic. (Robin Scholz/The News-Gazette)

Illinois
23
0

REGULAR SEASON
ILLINI 78, NEBRASKA 69

February 1, 2026

Red hot Illini win 11th in a row

Underwood leverages big lineups to beat Nebraska on the road

By **SCOTT RICHEY**
srichey@news-gazette.com

LINCOLN, Neb. — Illinois men's basketball has the biggest team in the country this season.

Taller, collectively, than the other 364 Division I teams.

Maybe you heard Brad Underwood discuss "positional size" a time or two this past offseason as his 2025-26 roster came together. It's what the Illini coach wanted and exactly what he got.

Losing Kylan Boswell to a broken bone in his right hand — at least for a while — basically means Illinois defaults to big lineups given the rotation hasn't changed other than going from eight-deep to seven.

Illinois leaned into its size advantage on Sunday afternoon against No. 5 Nebraska.

While Keaton Wagler and Jake Davis already tie as the shortest starter at 6-foot-6, the No. 9 Illini pushed the envelop on big lineups at various points to leverage that advantage even further against the Cornhuskers.

The biggest the lineup got? Wagler at the point joined by 6-9 Ben Humrichous, 6-9 David Mirkovic, 7-1 Tomislav Ivisic and 7-2 Zvonimir Ivisic.

Underwood sprinkled in other various big lineups throughout Sunday's game. The 6-4 Brandon Lee made it as far as the scorer's table in the first half before being pulled back to the bench by Underwood, meaning Wagler and Davis were the shortest Illinois players to see the court.

The result was a notable rebounding advantage, plenty of mismatches against smaller Nebraska lineups and still enough defense to withstand a flurry of first-half three-pointers by the 'Huskers for a 78-69 victory in front of 15,513 fans at Pinnacle Bank Arena.

An 11th straight win that kept Illinois (19-3, 10-1 Big Ten) perfect away from home in conference play this season. All with lineups few teams in the Big Ten — or nationally — could match up with all that effectively.

"It gives us some options, some opportunities, to really space it, but it also gives us the opportunity to play above people and over the top," Underwood said. "You throw a bunch of 6-9 to 7-2 guys out there, it gives us the chance to do that. Mirk gives us that luxury because of his ball-handling and his passing."

The lineup with the Ivisic twins, Mirkovic, Humrichous and Wagler had played 1 minute together this season before Sunday's game. That jumbo lineup — and the almost equally as big other options — caused trouble for Nebraska (20-2, 9-2).

The 'Huskers lost the rebounding battle by 13 and let Illinois turn 11 offensive rebounds into 10 second-chance points. The length of Illinois' big lineups also hamstrung the Nebraska offense. While the 'Huskers knocked down 15 of 35 three-pointers, they were just 10 of 24 on twos and missed five layups.

"I thought their length in the paint bothered us," Nebraska coach Fred Hoiberg said. "It took away some of our cutting. I thought early we curled, we got in there and we made some plays. We sprayed it out and had some really good looks (from three-point range). The second half we couldn't get those looks."

David Mirkovic drives inside against Nebraska forward Rienk Mast in the first half. (Associated Press)

NEBRASKA
51
B1G
FIGHTING
0
ILLINI

The big lineup worked out for Illinois on the offensive end, too. A main concept to the Illini's top-rated offense is matchup hunting. Going big, with five players who can all shoot, creates more mismatches.

"We just tried to manipulate the floor to be guarded by somebody we'd want in that moment," said Tomislav Ivisic, who finished Sunday's win with 12 points, eight rebounds and three assists.

Wagler was, in most of those lineups, the only guard on the court. The shortest player, too, which he said was definitely a rarity in his basketball career before he got to Champaign.

"There's a lot of mismatches when we have a tall lineup out there," the Illinois freshman guard said after dropping 28 points on Nebraska. "It just gives us a different look for offense and defense, and I think it's really cool to be able to play that at all of a lineup."

Illinois used those unique lineups to secure some redemption after its Dec. 13 loss to the 'Huskers in Champaign. Sunday's win also helped the Illini keep pace with Michigan at the top of the Big Ten standings.

That it was a second Big Ten road win against a Top 10 opponent in just more than a week after knocking off Purdue at Mackey Arena on Jan. 24 gave it even more meaning.

"The first loss at State Farm, we felt like we were a better team, but we just didn't play very well," Tomislav Ivisic said. "Since the loss of that game, we really went on a run. I wouldn't say we changed, but we adjusted our defense. Since then, we've just played with a lot of effort, a lot of tenacity. Now, beating them just proves we are the better team."

Underwood said Illinois has shown resilience in its 11-game winning streak. Shown poise with growing purpose and connectivity on the court. Outrebounding Nebraska 40-27 and taking the 'Huskers out of their offensive rhythm was also a difference-maker.

"We've been playing offense at a pretty good clip, and it's been different things," Underwood said. Sunday against the 'Huskers was getting to the free-throw line and points in the paint with the Illini shooting just 9 of 30 from three-point range.

"But you only win on the road if you can guard at a certain level and rebound at a certain level," the Illinois coach continued. "I think that's the one thing we've been able to do — at least in the last couple."

Ben Humrichous shoots a 3-point basket against Nebraska guard Jamarques Lawrence during the second half. (Associated Press)

GET LOUD
N
LANTZ 22
HOPPEN 42
PIATKOWSKI 52
LUE 10
Bryan Health
THE VAULT
Huskers
NEBRASKA 10
FIGHTING ILLINI 3
23
fnbo
Channel

REGULAR SEASON

MICHIGAN STATE 85, ILLINI 82 (OT)

February 7, 2026

Little mistakes add up

Illini look in charge throughout but cannot put Spartans away in overtime defeat

By SCOTT RICHEY
srichey@news-gazette.com

EAST LANSING, Mich. — Andrej Stojakovic walked off the court at the Breslin Center on Saturday night with his arm around Keaton Wagler's shoulders and a message to share.

Stojakovic has certainly seen more in his college career than his freshman teammate. A season at Stanford and another at California have imbued the veteran guard with some perspective Wagler simply can't have 24 games into his first season of college basketball at Illinois.

What played out Saturday night in East Lansing, Mich., was new for Wagler.

Facing a Top 10 team on the road in Big Ten play? That he'd done.

Twice. To impressive results. But Saturday against Michigan State was different.

The Spartans did their level best to contain Wagler, and while he still put up 16 points, it came on 16 shots.

Inefficiency the 6-foot-6 freshman hadn't really dealt with this season. Particularly not on the road in the Big Ten where he's actually been at his best.

Wagler wasn't at his best Saturday against Michigan State. Neither was No. 5 Illinois as a whole, with a series of little mistakes adding up to an 85-82 overtime loss to the No. 10 Spartans in front of a near capacity crowd of 14,797.

"I just let him know that all he can do is learn," Stojakovic said of his discussion with Wagler walking off the court. "You can't change anything about the outcome of the game. Hopefully, we'll see them back. That's a great team. We want to play them again."

Wagler's rough night still almost included a spectacular comeback after he knocked down a deep three-pointer with six seconds to play in overtime and stole the inbounds pass to give the Illini a shot to send Saturday's game into a second overtime. Zvonimir Ivisic's off-balance three-pointer from the top of the key was too long and hit off the backboard as the buzzer sounded.

"Because of those previous 50/50 plays and offensive rebounds, I don't think we deserved to hit that shot," Illinois forward David Mirkovic said.

Those would be the minor mistakes sprinkled throughout Saturday night's game that individually wouldn't have been an issue, but cumulatively kept Illinois from extending its Big Ten-leading winning streak. Michigan State outrebounded the Illini 48-38, and while the offensive rebounds were even, the Spartans' managed second-chance opportunities in key late-game moments to end a 12-game win streak for Illinois (20-4, 11-2 Big Ten).

Points in the paint favored Michigan State (20-4, 10-3).

So did fast-break points.

So did bench points.

But it was the rebounding advantage and hustle plays that were the difference between Illinois' 13th straight win and their first loss in nearly two months.

"They've just pulverized some teams on the boards," Michigan State coach Tom Izzo said. "We put all of our efforts into that, and I think we did a decent job of that. That was probably the difference in the game. ... That's a better team than we are right now — especially going into this game. They had won 12 in a row, and we were limping."

Andrej Stojakovic shoots against Michigan State guard Kur Teng. (Associated Press)

Illinois
2

REGULAR SEASON
ILLINI 71, INDIANA 51

February 15, 2026

Back with a vengeance

Boswell's return as impactful as expected as Illini rout Hoosiers at home

By SCOTT RICHEY
srichey@news-gazette.com

CHAMPAIGN — Kylan Boswell was ready to play.

More than ready, really, after missing seven games because of a broken bone in his right hand.

That was particularly true watching his Illinois men's basketball team drop back-to-back overtime games in a row after the winning streak he left at seven was pushed to 12 in his absence. Moments he felt like he could help the team fend off Michigan State or Wisconsin stung with him planted on the bench.

So, Thursday's all-clear from the doctors to play on Sunday afternoon against Indiana was embraced. It marked the end of his return-to-play process, which included a slow, but steady ramp-up of contact in practice in the last week-and-half.

But there was still a bit of trepidation from Boswell — a little worry — about how his hand would hold up in a game.

Confidence for Boswell came in the form of a recent Illinois All-American. The timing of the NBA All-Star break and the Illinois senior guard's return couldn't have been better.

Terrence Shannon Jr. spent several days this past week back in Champaign. That included time on the court Friday and Saturday on the Illinois scout team, giving his best Lamar Wilkerson impression to help the Illini prepare for the high-scoring Hoosiers' guard.

"(Shannon) was helpful the last two days for me, for sure," Boswell said. "Being able to guard him and him guarding me throughout practice definitely helped my confidence."

Confidence that delivered all you might expect with Boswell back on the court for Illinois.

A big pop from another sold-out State Farm Center crowd when he was the final starter announced before the game. Plenty of defense, with Wilkerson his primary target. And another fill-the-gaps, do-a-little-bit-of-everything performance.

Boswell might not have been Illinois' leading scorer — or even Nos. 2 or 3 on that list — but his presence and productivity on the court was crucial in a 71-51 blowout win for No. 8 Illinois against Indiana.

"I just think getting a focus — a mental focus — was probably the important piece of that," Illinois coach Brad Underwood said. "He's a tough, tough, tough sucker. He got his appointment moved up. He pushed for that. Everything's right in his hand, and that dude was ready to be back in a jersey and perform. I was very happy the crowd acknowledged him. We're a better team for having him on the court."

Boswell broke the bone in his right hand during a Jan. 19 practice at Ubben Basketball Complex and had surgery that same week to pin and plate the break. While Underwood said he anticipated a mid-February return, Boswell always thought his first game back would be Wednesday night against Southern Cal in Los Angeles.

Boswell's quicker-than-expected return to play was result of several factors. Lots of time in the hyperbaric chamber and infrared sauna at Ubben plus regular bone stimulation certainly helped. He also prioritized sleep to fast forward the healing process.

Kylan Boswell — back in action after missing seven games with a broken bone in his hand — drives against Indiana's Tucker DeVries. (Robin Scholz/The News-Gazette)

Illinois
4
INDIANA
1

"The biggest thing was the swelling," Boswell said. "I didn't want to be out there with my hand swelling up, but that went down and the doctor took a look a the X-rays and none of the screws were moving around after practice the first couple weeks. It was definitely a fast process, but I was grateful for that."

Gratitude was top of mind for Boswell following Sunday's big win by the Illini (21-5, 12-3 Big Ten) against the Hoosiers (17-9, 8-7). For the response he got from the crowd during the starting lineup introductions.

For his teammates making his return an easy one.

David Mirkovic scored a game-high 25 points to go with seven rebounds and three assists. Keaton Wagler added 18 points, six rebounds, three assists and three steals, and Tomislav Ivisic made it three in double figures with 14 points and six rebounds.

Boswell didn't have to automatically be the end-all, be-all for Illinois in his first game back.

But his contributions of nine points, seven rebounds and two assists were good enough when coupled with the spark he gave his team on the defensive end of the court.

"Kylan is our most important player — especially on the defensive end," Mirkovic said. "The biggest thing from (Sunday) having him back, I feel safer with him on the court guarding the other (team's) best players."

That's where Indiana coach Darian DeVries noticed Boswell's effect. The Hoosiers anticipated Boswell playing Sunday given the word out of Ubben throughout the week, and even though Wilkerson scored a team-high 21 points, it wasn't an easy 21.

"The biggest thing with him is his defensive ability that he brings — his physicality to chase guys around," DeVries said. "I thought he did a good job of making things hard for Lamar a lot of the time. What he brings and adds to the team in his return is another defensive guy who can be that shutdown guy."

Boswell played Sunday with his right hand well padded and wrapped. It's a bit bothersome since that is his shooting hand — and probably contributed to a couple missed layups — but he said his only choice is to accept it and move forward.

"Whatever the case may be, if it's not going offensively, I'll do my best to do other things to help my team win," Boswell said. "There's opportunities for me to make impactful plays without the ball in my hands. I think I've done a great job with that my two years being here."

ABOVE: Ben Humrichous and David Mirkovic (0) double up on Indiana's Lamar Wilkerson. (Robin Scholz/The News-Gazette)

RIGHT: The Orange Krush fans celebrate after Illinois center Zvonimir Ivisic dunks. (Robin Scholz/The News-Gazette)

Illinois
44
ILLINOIS
FIGHTING

REGULAR SEASON
MICHIGAN 84, ILLINI 70

February 27, 2026

Another lesson to learn

Underwood looking for 'nastiness' from Illini after defeat

By SCOTT RICHEY
srichey@news-gazette.com

CHAMPAIGN — The disappointment radiated off Kylan Boswell during his postgame press conference Friday night at State Farm Center.

Boswell put voice to his frustration in the wake of Illinois' 84-70 loss to Michigan, but it wasn't necessary.

Body language. Tone. The look in his eyes.

That told the story as much as anything the veteran Illini guard could say about the way the Wolverines simply dominated the game. A realization, in one of the final days of February, that the window for a game like that not to be a crushing blow to a season was shrinking.

Two regular-season games remain for No. 10 Illinois (22-6, 13-4 Big Ten) before the conference tournament in Chicago. A win-or-go-home scenario one step below the win-or-your-season-is-over NCAA tournament.

Boswell has experienced that each of the past three seasons. Twice at Arizona and then again last season in first at Illinois. That's firsthand knowledge about how a performance like Friday against Michigan can bring about the abrupt end in tournament play.

Friday didn't mark Illinois' first February loss, but what happened against Michigan was different. The three overtime losses before it came with a sense of the Illini beating themselves. Reasonable considering they were in position to win all three before squandering leads against Michigan State, Wisconsin and UCLA.

"It's been a while since we've played a team that beat us for sure," Boswell said. "We've got to remember this feeling because two more games from now there's no more opportunities, really, and you've got to take care of business the first time.

"I'm so frustrated at myself and disappointed in how I played. I feel like I let us down. I can't afford that type of stuff for this team. These guys lean on me."

Brad Underwood is going to lean on Boswell to get Illinois back on track. The same with Tomislav Ivisic, Ben Humrichous and Jake Davis. They've all been through a full season in Champaign.

But the challenge from Underwood will extend beyond his veteran core after Friday's loss to Michigan. Not so much for the result itself — the Wolverines are the outright Big Ten champions for a reason — but for how a competitive game fell apart in the second half. How Illinois' deficit ballooned to 21 points before Michigan closed out its road win.

"The lesson was learned," Underwood said. "(Michigan) took the belt off and beat our behinds with it."

A result that happened, in Underwood's estimation, because his team got too content with its successes. A little complacent over time. What was a 12-game winning streak from Braggin' Rights in late December through sweeping the season series with Northwestern at the beginning of February has turned into four losses in six games.

Right before March.

"That's on me," Underwood said. "Look no further than the guy sitting up here letting that happen. It always catches you at some point. It smacks you in the face and doesn't feel very good. I don't like saying that about my team very often, but (Michigan) played harder than we did. They played nastier than we did."

The Krush section tries to distract Michigan's guard Elliot Cadeau during a free throw attempt. (Robin Scholz/The News-Gazette)

CADEAU
3
23
FIGHTING
32
ILLINI
MONTENEGRO
FIGHTING
11
ILLINI
ORANGE
6
KRUSH
BARK
SNA
TOYOTA

REGULAR SEASON

ILLINI 80, OREGON 54

March 3, 2026

Challenge accepted

Stojakovic shines in Big Ten blowout

By SCOTT RICHEY
srichey@news-gazette.com

CHAMPAIGN — Brad Underwood couldn't have been more clear about what he needed from Andrej Stojakovic in the wake of last week's home loss to Michigan.

Underwood laid it out in simple terms. Stojakovic's going scoreless against the Wolverines certainly wasn't ideal, but the Illinois coach took significantly more issue with the single rebound from the 6-foot-7 guard.

Stojakovic's struggles against Michigan didn't single him out. Rebounding and defense was a team-wide issue in the 84-70 loss to the Big Ten champs. But Stojakovic at his best can be a game changer for Illinois.

That wasn't the case last Friday. Two impressive practices carrying over into Tuesday night's game against Oregon was a different story.

Underwood challenged Stojakovic in the two days leading into No. 11 Illinois' regular season home finale. The veteran guard responded with 21 points, 12 rebounds and a pair of assists — all in just 21 minutes — to lead the Illini to an 80-54 victory.

A "get right" game for Illinois and Stojakovic both.

"I love the fact I challenged him, and he responded," Underwood said. "Andrej is so coachable. I said, 'We need 10 rebounds from you.' When he rebounds at a high level, we get some easy baskets in transition. It's a really important piece for us. He provides that. When you get 12 rebounds in (21) minutes, you're chasing it. My hat's off to him."

Stojakovic said it was only natural to question a lot about what went wrong against Michigan. He was frustrated with how he played. That he wasn't himself. Certainly not his best self.

Conversations with Underwood and the Illinois coaching staff — discussions that helped to emphasis his role — were critical in the lead up to Tuesday's game against Oregon.

"I think to stick with coach's plan that he had for me was the most important thing," Stojakovic said. "The practices that I had carried over to the game — the defense, the rebounding on both sides. Just trust the process. There's going to be highs and lows.

"We've talked about an adjusted role from my previous years. Obviously, for any confident player it's going to be tough. It's staying mentally strong knowing at the end of the day the coach is going to need each player to do what they do in order to win. Really hearing the staff out and the game plan, that was most important."

Those conversations between player and coach included some constructive criticism. Some critiques.

"He's not a guy you've got to rip his tail and get on him, but you have to challenge him," Underwood said. "It's conversation. He's got a tremendous amount of pride, and I think he understands his value to our team. I think he understands what winning is looking like maybe a lot more than he did at some point in his time here.

"I don't think he's ever doubted his abilities or what he's capable of, but (Tuesday) was a great night for him. It started with his effort and his work in practice. He

Fans react to a basket by the Illini's Kylan Boswell during a home blowout win over Oregon. (Robin Scholz/The News-Gazette)

Illinois
ORANGE
6
KRUSH
Illinois
4
ILLINOIS

was dominating practice. I always love to see really good players dominate practice."

Stojakovic said he didn't lose his confidence "in any way" with his struggles against Michigan, where he played a career low 12 minutes. Re-establishing his assertiveness against Oregon was key. That came both with a focus on rebounding and defense and a one-track mind on getting to the rim.

Oregon had no answer for Stojakovic's dribble drives. Other than fouling. His game-high 21 points came on 7 of 12 shooting from the field and a perfect 7 of 7 mark at the free throw line.

"The thing I like, what he does best, is not just finish, but I like his passing," Underwood said. "He's doing a great job and really improving in that area in spraying it because teams have to collapse. It puts foul pressure on teams. He's a very good free throw shooter. ... He maybe takes one or two mid-range, but most of those things are right at the rim, and that opens things up for our perimeter guys."

Illinois shot 10 of 36 from three-point win in Tuesday's win. Stojakovic's first assist led to a Jake Davis' lone make from the perimeter.

"We have a lot of shooters on our team," Illinois forward David Mirkovic said. "It's really important to have someone who can dunk on someone every game. ... He's just got to keep practicing the way he did and for that to carry over into the games."

RIGHT: Andrej Stojakovic reacts while hanging on the rim after a dunk against Oregon. (Robin Scholz/The News-Gazette)

FACING: Illinois guard Brandon Lee drives to the basket against the Ducks. (Robin Scholz/The News-Gazette)

Illinois
1

The bench reacts to a basket and a foul for Illinois guard AJ Redd against Oregon. (Robin Scholz/The News-Gazette)

Illinois
3
Illinois
44

Boswell closing out on his terms

By SCOTT RICHEY
srichey@news-gazette.com

CHAMPAIGN — It was a freak practice accident.

Kylan Boswell was guarding Mihailo Petrovic aggressively. No surprise there. Then Boswell's finger got caught on Petrovic's forearm and snapped back.

That's all it took for Boswell to know, in an instant, that he had broken a bone in his hand. Seven years earlier, he suffered the same injury — same spot, same break — as an eighth-grader at Urbana Middle School, and that's all the Illinois men's basketball team's guard could think about on that Monday in late January at Ubben Basketball Complex.

Boswell flashed back to that initial injury. Not necessarily to the pain, but more to the months — plural — it took for the break to heal.

"I thought I was out for the season," Boswell told The News-Gazette. "I didn't think about surgery, though, in that moment when I broke it because I just remembered how long it took me to come back (in eighth grade) because I let it heal naturally. It took me a month-and-a-half to two months before I even started to try dribbling again."

You know the story from there. Boswell had surgery that same week, which included inserting a plate and pins into his hand to stabilize the bones. Surgery that cut his recovery to less than a month. Boswell missed seven games, returned to action Feb. 15 against Indiana and helped Illinois close out the regular season with four wins in six games to secure the No. 4 seed and triple bye in the Big Ten tournament that is now underway at the United Center in Chicago.

It's a reality, though, Boswell didn't consider in the immediate aftermath of the injury. The Champaign native was certain his senior season at Illinois had been snatched out from underneath him.

"I was thinking in my head, 'There's no way this just happened right now,'" Boswell said. "I was playing really well. We were on a roll at the time. I started crying in the hospital room — sad, very frustrated and upset. I was overwhelmed with emotions."

Then came the best-case scenario from Boswell's doctor. The previous break with its regrown bone would actually help with the healing process the second time around. After surgery, of course.

That was relief for Boswell, tinged with some apprehension. Having already undergone a previous surgery on his foot, he wasn't thrilled with the idea of going under the knife again. Boswell knew it would expedite his return to the court, but wrapping his head around surgery required some introspection.

"I did not like the idea," Boswell said. "I, at first, was huge on board with letting it heal naturally. But I broke the same bone in eighth grade and I don't ever want to have another problem like this, so I think the best decision was surgery. We just had to get it done."

The alternative was likely never suiting up for Illinois again, which would have been giving up a lot. Not just the end of his college basketball career, but the end of a promising season with realistic postseason goals still left to achieve.

That's a reality Boswell didn't want to consider.

Kylan Boswell poses during the Illini's preseason media day. (Robin Scholz/The News-Gazette)

"The team really wanted me to be out there in the timeframe I was gone," he said. "I think the best version of ourselves as a team is if I'm able to play and be on the court. I just couldn't really grasp the idea of not being able to finish out this year or that concept of just not playing."

Brandon Boswell called the broken bone in his son's hand "a heartbreak" and "a tough pill to swallow" when it happened. How they handled the injury as a family — particularly from his son's end — was important.

"At the end of the day, they know who you are if they're interested in you at the next level," Brandon Boswell said. "Then you've got to know who you are to make sure you come back and help the program that you're in right now. Make sure that that's your goal."

Boswell slid right back into Illinois' starting lineup when he made his return against Indiana. The 6-foot-2 guard had nine points, seven rebounds and two assists in the Illini's 71-51 win. More than the production, though, he brought back a steady hand and calming presence to the court.

Boswell's overall production has dipped in the six games after his return to averaging 10.5 points on 40/29/71 shooting to go with 3.5 rebounds and 3.5 assists per game. Pre-injury, Boswell averaged 14.3 points on 47/31/82 shooting along with 4.2 rebounds and 3.4 assists per game in slightly more playing time.

But Boswell's value goes beyond his counting stats. That's something his teammates expressed repeatedly in the immediate aftermath of his injury and upon his return. The Champaign native is their leader.

"He never missed a beat in terms of his commitment and dedication to our program," Illinois coach Brad Underwood said about how Boswell handled his injury. "He's a great, great competitor, and he cares about winning at a really high level. His impact on us has been just that. That's been the greatest attribute. What he's done physically and on the court has been, obviously, very impactful, but it's his competitive spirit, his unselfishness."

Boswell has basketball ambitions beyond Champaign, but those can wait. The 20-year-old has tried to stay in the moment — enjoy his final season at home — and not think too much about what's next. Doing so earlier in this career got him in trouble.

"When I first ever started seeing my name on draft boards my sophomore year, I put a lot of pressure on myself," Boswell said. "I think that completely derailed my game — my confidence, my mental state. As I've gotten older, just being more calm and even-keeled and just being myself and putting the work in, good things will happen.

"I think whatever falls into place for my life and whatever my situation is after this season ends, I feel like I'm confident and comfortable in where I'll be. I believe that I'll be in the NBA. I believe I'll be somebody who can be impactful for a team."

The good things Boswell wants now are for Illinois. The Big Ten tournament is important — the Illini want to win — but there's also a realization that the NCAA tournament will follow. Boswell can see a "huge run" in his team's future.

"Every day we talk about leveraging one another, playing for each other," he said. "Everybody understands what they do best, and we fall into that role just being able to help one another become the best version of ourselves on this team. I'm really excited for when March Madness starts."

Kylan Boswell is fouled by UTRGV's forward Kye Dickson during a game in November. (Robin Scholz/The News-Gazette)

ILLINOIS
B1G

The Orange Krush fans take in the action during a regular-season game against Wisconsin at the State Farm Center. (Robin Scholz/The News-Gazette)

Tomislav Ivisic goofs around with Ty Rodgers (20) while Keaton Wagler smiles and Brandon Lee ignores them during the preseason media day. (Robin Scholz/The News-Gazette)

From left, Andrej Stojakovic, Ben Humrichous, Tomislav Ivisic, Zvonimir Ivisic and Jason Jakstys try to keep straight faces while posing for their team photo. (Robin Scholz/The News-Gazette)

Former Illinois players Will Riley, left, and Kasparas Jakucionis chat with associate head coach Orlando Antigua before a home game against Indiana. (Robin Scholz/The News-Gazette)

The fans at State Farm Center use the flashlights on thier phones during introductions before the Illini play host to Southern. (Robin Scholz/The News-Gazette)

20:00
ILLINOIS

Fans at the State Farm Center in an "Orange Out" before the game against Northwestern. (Robin Scholz/The News-Gazette)

ILLINOIS
120
ILLINI

BIG TEN TOURNAMENT
WISCONSIN 91, ILLINI 88 (OT)

March 13, 2026

Unexpected setback

Short stint in Chicago wasn't the plan for Illini

By SCOTT RICHEY
srichey@news-gazette.com

CHICAGO — The mood in the Illinois men's basketball team's locker room early Friday evening at the United Center went beyond appropriately somber.

Frustration. Disappointment and disbelief. Truly a sense of "What just happened?"

A reasonable reaction to a 15-point second-half lead disappearing in a Nick Boyd and John Blackwell flurry. To a second overtime loss to Wisconsin roughly a month after the first. To a short stay at the Big Ten tournament in the wake of that 91-88 loss to the Badgers that needed a bonus five minutes to decide in front of 18,988 fans.

"This wasn't a scenario in my head," Illinois center Tomislav Ivisic said. "I thought we were going to go to the finals, fight for the championship, because I felt we were good enough for that. First loss here is not what we expected, but it is what it is.

"It's sport. It's basketball. One team wins, and one team loses. We've got to get ready, clear our heads and do what we can because our season is not over. We've got the most important part coming. If we do good, nobody is going to talk about what happened before."

The NCAA tournament will give No. 9 Illinois (24-8) a second chance at a postseason run, but Friday's loss to No. 23 Wisconsin (24-9) can't be easily pushed aside. Not after a 28-13 lead in the first half was whittled to 36-30 by halftime. Not after the Badgers did it again in the second half, riding a wave of Boyd and Blackwell dribble drives — and their 69 total points — to a come-from-behind victory. Illinois led Wisconsin 60-45 with 11:34 left in the second half. A little more than minutes later, the Illini only led 62-60 with 7:03 remaining.

Big leads for Illinois that weren't big enough. An all-too-familiar scenario in the last month-plus during overtime losses against Michigan State, Wisconsin, UCLA and, now, Wisconsin again.

"The biggest thing was just the loss of focus when we had our lead," Illinois guard Kylan Boswell said. "You can't really go six minutes without scoring with a 15-point lead, let the team come back and think you're going to win. Momentum is completely on their side. That's the biggest thing about this sport. Momentum will kill you. If we want to win these games, get past the second round (in the NCAA tournament), we can't let that type of stuff happen."

The lingering frustration — the disappointment and disbelief for Illinois — was rooted in the fact that Wisconsin comeback didn't have to happen. Momentum might have materialized on the Badgers' side in the second half, but there were opportunities to flip it again.

"It's definitely hard, but it's not impossible," Ivisic said. "If we play hard, if we talk, if we rebound — if we do everything we did in the first half — I think we would have won the game. We just need to be locked in for 40 minutes. We cannot have some possessions that we play hard and the next one we don't. One possession we crash (the boards rebounding) and the next possession we don't."

Illinois also couldn't let Boyd and Blackwell change the game the way they did. The Wisconsin duo combined for 50 points in the second half and overtime.

Illinois center Zvonimir Ivisic dunks during the Big Ten Tournament against Wisconsin. (Robin Scholz/The News-Gazette)

Part competitor, part goofball

By SCOTT RICHEY
srichey@news-gazette.com

DAVID MIRKOVIC WASN'T ABOUT to let the flu keep him off the court in January at Northwestern.

An ankle injury before the Illinois men's basketball team faced Purdue was treated the same way for the same reason.

Mirkovic couldn't stand even the thought his team might take a loss if he didn't play when there was even a chance he could. So, he got a pregame IV to make it through a road win against the Wildcats and played through pain for another against the Boilermakers.

It wasn't even really a question. If Mirkovic was upright, he was going to play.

A level of sheer competitiveness that took on a different level when Mirkovic sent a text to Illinois coach Brad Underwood after the Illini lost an overtime game at home to Wisconsin. The 6-foot-9 freshman forward wasn't the only one who struggled against the Badgers, but his lengthy missive to Underwood was about taking responsibility and shouldering the blame.

"His competitive fire burns," Underwood said. "It hurts him. We've all grown up in locker rooms — or I did — and when you lost, there were tears and there were holes in the walls. This culture is not quite wired that way, but that one is."

That's just half of the equation. Only part of what makes Mirkovic who he is. The other half? That's the Mirkovic who decided, in the moment, that an underhand, full-court pass in Illinois' season opener against Jackson State on Nov. 3 at State Farm Center in Champaign was a good idea. Then, he unabashedly said after that game he might do it again.

"Yes, I'm surprised I haven't seen it again, but, yeah, it's a good thing we haven't seen it again," Illinois forward Ben Humrichous said with a smile on Wednesday afternoon. "A lot of self control on his part."

Part ultra competitor. Part goofball. The full Mirkovic experience. A combination that's proven vital in Illinois' success so far this season and will remain so as NCAA tournament play starts. The third-seeded Illini (24-8) face 14th-seeded Penn (18-11) in a first-round game at 8:25 p.m. on Thursday from Bon Secours Wellness Arena in Greenville, S.C.

"That's the beauty of Mirk," Underwood said. "What you see is what you get, but you know and understand his competitive drive never stops. It is full bore every play and in every drill. Part of what makes him good is his ability to go make plays and have that freedom — that artistic side, maybe — to his brute physicality. It's kind of a relief. It took a little while for me to adjust, but I actually enjoy him. He's one of the funniest human beings on this planet."

That's something Zvonimir Ivisic first recognized six years ago when he first met Mirkovic. The two were teammates long before they wound up together at Illinois, and it was Ivisic's presence in Champaign — along with his twin brother, Tomislav — that made the Illini the one and only college basketball program the Niksic, Montenegro, native would consider.

"Since he was 14, always goofy, hilarious," Zvonimir Ivisic said about Mirkovic. "Always

David Mirkovic poses during the Illini's preseason media day. (Rob LeCates/The News-Gazette)

B1G
ILLINOIS
0

finds himself in, I'm not going to say trouble, but some hilarious situations that only he can find himself in.

"His game is way better than I've ever seen before, but he's still got his personality. I don't think he's ever going to change that. I think that's a good thing about him. That keeps him going. That gives him confidence."

Confidence that, as competitive as Mirkovic is, needed the occasional boost throughout the season. A reminder from his teammates not about how good the freshman forward could be, but how good he already was. Particularly when his competitiveness turned into too much critical self-reflection.

"Sometimes, he can get hard on himself, but we are all confident in what David can do," Humrichous said. "Sometimes, it's just like, 'Dude, go get a bucket. You're really good at what you do. Remember you're really good at what you do. Go get a bucket or go make the right play and continue to be you.'"

That's where Mirkovic said he's grown the most from a mental standpoint. That it was OK to be himself.

"This season was really helpful for me," Mirkovic said. "I gained a lot of experience, and I learned a lot about college basketball and American basketball. I would say I learned I've got to play more confident and more aggressive. Be yourself. Play like you played when you were 10 years old. Don't think about mistakes because mistakes are normal."

Mirkovic also learned how to harness his competitive nature and carefree spirit into a potent combination for Illinois this season. The All-Big Ten Freshman Team selection and honorable-mention All-Big Ten pick enters the NCAA tournament averaging 13.4 points on 49/37/79 shooting to go with 7.8 rebounds and 2.6 assists per game. The Illini's leading rebounder, second-leading scorer and third-leading facilitator.

Not to mention full-time vibes leader.

"As a competitor, so much of his spirit resonates throughout our team," Illinois assistant coach Tyler Underwood said. "He has grown a lot. A lot of times, his emotions would get the better of him early in the season. There would be inflection points where it's like, 'I don't know if we can keep him in the game because he's fouling, because he's emotional.'

"His emotional growth has helped this team a great deal. I think it speaks to his character and competitiveness that he wants to work on those things. He's an unbelievable basketball player and unbelievable competitor, and has such a bright career ahead of him."

Mirkovic's competitive fire is something he came by naturally. His mom, Jelena, played professional basketball and represented Yugoslavia internationally. His approach to the game and his drive to win is a product of her own competitiveness.

Leaving home wasn't easy for Mirkovic — and there were times homesickness kicked in the past nine months — but his family ultimately understood the opportunity that college basketball, that Illinois, presented.

"I knew that this was my path — the best path for me and the best option for me basketball-wise," Mirkovic said. "They were a little sad because I was going on the other side of the world, but I just told them that, 'I'm a grown man. I'm 20 years old. I've got to find my job.'"

A job he's excelled in this season for the Illini. All while matching that inner competitor and outer goofball.

"David will always have a little bit of little kid in him in all that we do," Humrichous said. "Even in practice, in a heated moment, he'll try to throw the ball off the top of the clock to see if he can make it in. That's just who he is, but, at the same time, when we get on the court and we're playing, he presents an intensity. When he really gets going, he presents a physicality that's not kid like."

David Mirkovic grabs the ball surrounded by Maryland players. (Robin Scholz/The News-Gazette)

MARYLAND
24
Illinois
0

NCAA FIRST ROUND
ILLINI 105, PENN 70

March 19, 2026

Domination from the outset

Mirkovic sets the tone in opening-round blowout

By SCOTT RICHEY
srichey@news-gazette.com

GREENVILLE, S.C. — David Mirkovic walked off the court at Bon Secours Wellness Arena for the last time during Thursday night's game against Penn with just more than 5 minutes to play.

There was nothing left for Mirkovic to do. Certainly nothing left to prove. Not after 29 points and 17 rebounds.

Zvonimir Ivisic was the first to reach Mirkovic, waiting for his longtime teammate with a hug. Assistant coach Orlando Antigua couldn't keep the smile off his face as he wrapped up Mirkovic as soon as he reached the bench.

The congratulations continued as Mirkovic made his way from one end of the bench to the other. All while he received boisterous cheers and applause from the Illinois fans closest to the team.

A standing ovation both deserved because of how Mirkovic dominated and the default option at that moment. The Illini fans were already on their feet as Thursday night's first-round NCAA tournament game turned into a blowout.

A 105-70 victory that sends Illinois into the second round for the third straight season. Up next? A 6:50 p.m. Saturday showdown with VCU.

But that's for Saturday.

Thursday night was for celebrating Mirkovic and one of the best games of his career. His 29 points set a new career high while also setting a new program record for most points by a freshman in an NCAA tournament game. His 17 rebounds didn't quite match the 21 he pulled down in November against Colgate, but they were the most by any Illinois player — ever — in March Madness.

"It's nothing new for him," Illinois guard Kylan Boswell said.

"He's such a physical guy, and he's always in the right positions at the right time. We give him the ball — him and Keaton (Wagler) — and tell them to basically just go dominate the game like they usually do. All the work they've put in, all the moments they've risen to the occasion throughout the year, this is nothing new for us."

Mirkovic secured his eighth double-double before halftime. His physicality set the tone early in the game, and his teammates fed on it. That came in the form of Tomislav Ivisic's 12 points and seven rebounds as a frontcourt complement, Ben Humrichous making 4 of 8 three-pointers, Boswell putting up an efficient 13 points and Wagler flirting with a triple-double with 18 points, seven rebounds and seven assists.

"He set the tone from the beginning," Zvonimir Ivisic said. "We saw him, and everybody started being more physical. He brings a lot of energy. He brings everything offensively and even defensively. He's a really important piece for us."

Brad Underwood said he can usually tell which version of Mirkovic he's going to get — how well the freshman forward will play — based on how he practices. It was all positive signs this week.

"I can usually tell in practice when he's at mentally in terms of being dialed in and focused," the Illinois coach said. "(Thursday) there were no distractions. He was good in

Tomislav Ivisic controls the ball against the Penn defense during a first-round NCAA Tournament victory. (Rob Le Cates/The News-Gazette)

Illinois
PENN
Ivy

the last 3-4 practices, and that carried over.

"When you step on the floor, he just wants to rip your head off. That's if you're officiating. That's if you're coaching him. He's just got an edge that's a competitive spirit that's unmatched."

Mirkovic's performance meant a postgame interview with sideline reporter Tracy Wolfson. Humrichous and Zvonimir Ivisic provided moral support, with Humrichous also on hand — both he and Mirkovic joked — for any necessary translator duties.

"Incredibly proud of him," Humrichous said about his freshman teammate. "A guy that can flip a switch and just do incredible things. I'm proud of the way he showed up physically on the glass and the effort that he made on a lot of plays. He deserves an awesome night like (Thursday)."

"Early in the game when you see how hard he's playing you just know good things are going to happen," Wagler added. "We send two people at him every time (in practice) to box him out because of how hard he goes. We barely call any fouls in practice, so we're fouling him and trying to stop him every time. He'll get mad — he wants a foul call — and I just think it makes it a lot tougher for him in practice and easier in games."

Mirkovic was proud to have set a couple of new Illinois records in NCAA tournament action. Certainly, happy he had played a key role in Thursday's blowout win. But he didn't get carried away by the moment.

It might have been the first round of the NCAA tournament, but Mirkovic said he treated it like any of the other 32 games he played this season.

"I was just going for rebounds," Mirkovic said. "I just felt basketballs were coming like magnets. That's because I crashed. I got a lot of open looks at the rim. That's what got me going and what got our team going.

"I know what I'm capable of. I know my good things, my bad things. I'm excited, of course, but we have our next game in less than 48 hours. We've just got to be focused and locked in for the next game."

David Mirkovic celebrates with Keaton Wagler during a first-round NCAA Tournament win over Penn. (Associated Press)

WAGLER

Stojakovic gets all he wanted

By **SCOTT RICHEY**
srichey@news-gazette.com

GREENVILLE, S.C. — Brad Underwood spent Selection Sunday enjoying how much fun Andrej Stojakovic was having.

The Illinois men's basketball team gathered at Ubben Basketball Complex in Champaign for the selection show. The Beef House Restaurant catered their dinner. David Mirkovic brought some special homemade Balkan dishes his sister made for everyone to try.

No uncertainty about if the Illini were in the 68-team NCAA tournament field. Illinois was a lock to see its name when the brackets were revealed. A No. 3 seed after winning 24 games in the regular season and finishing in the top four in the Big Ten followed.

Plenty to celebrate.

But Stojakovic's joy came from a deeper place. Playing on an NCAA tournament team was a primary motivating factor when he left California after the 2024-25 season.

The Golden Bears finished 14-19 overall. Their 6-14 record landed them at 15th in their first season in the ACC.

It wasn't much different than Stojakovic's freshman year at Stanford. The Cardinal posted a 14-18 record and won just eight games for a ninth-place finish in the Pac-12 in what turned out to be Jerod Haase's final season as coach.

Stojakovic wanted more from his college basketball experience. Illinois provided the more.

"He was a kid in the candy store," Underwood said about how Stojakovic treated Selection Sunday. "He was the first one there. He was the first one through the food line. He was the first one seated. That's what he came here for — to understand that feeling and what this is about. You don't take this for granted."

Wednesday in Greenville created some new lasting memories for Stojakovic. Stepping on the NCAA and March Madness-branded court at Bon Secours Wellness Arena ahead of Illinois' open shootaround was "the moment that really got" him.

Thursday night was different. Both just another game while doubling as the highest stakes game of Stojakovic's college basketball career to that point.

Illinois' 105-70 victory against Penn finally gave Stojakovic some ammunition in a friendly back and forth with teammate Kylan Boswell about their respective NCAA tournament careers.

Another win Saturday night against VCU — with a spot in the Sweet 16 on the line — would provide even more.

"He has made it four years in a row and this is my first time, but I told him that so far I'm undefeated in this tournament and he isn't," Stojakovic said with a laugh. "I'm going to have that on him."

Some of Stojakovic's teammates are also experiencing the NCAA tournament for the first time. It's different, though, for freshmen Keaton Wagler, David Mirkovic and Brandon Lee. They've never even had the opportunity. Stojakovic has already played two seasons that failed to produce that result.

How much Stojakovic is enjoying his time in Greenville hasn't just struck Underwood. The junior guard's teammates see it, too.

"It's so much fun," said Illinois forward

Andrej Stojakovic poses during the Illini's preseason media day. (Rob LeCates/The News-Gazette)

BIG
ILLINOIS
2

Ben Humrichous, who went through a similar situation last season with the Illini after one season at Evansville and three at Huntington University. Last year's two-game stint in Milwaukee, Wis., was his first in the NCAA tournament.

"I told Dre (on Thursday) when he got on the bus, I'm smiling because of how much fun he's having," Humrichous continued. "I remember what that feeling was like. I don't ever want to take that for granted. Seeing that on Andrej's face (Thursday) night, his realization of what had just transpired, it gives you that extra boost."

An NCAA tournament appearance wasn't guaranteed when Stojakovic committed to Illinois last April, but the program's reputation shift in Underwood's tenure as coach was appealing. So were the teammates he'd get to play with, including 7-foot twins Tomislav and Zvonimir Ivisic. The emergence of Wagler and Mirkovic was "a pleasant surprise along the way" as they've played as crucial a role in Illinois' success this season as anyone.

It's everything Stojakovic wanted. A program that would challenge him and develop his game and a program he could help elevate to a higher level. A goal Stojakovic and the Illini are chasing in Greenville.

"That's the beauty of Andrej is how coachable he is and how he's starving for success and what that looks like — on all fronts," Underwood said. "Not just the individual success, but the team success."

Underwood didn't take it easy on Stojakovic. A knee injury might have kept the 6-foot-7 guard sidelined in the fall, changing the timeline for how the Illinois coach could challenge him to be more than a high-level scorer, but that idea never disappeared.

Eliciting Stojakovic's best defense and rebounding self was always the goal.

"I think I knew what I was getting into when I was coming to play for Brad," Stojakovic said. "Obviously, a hard-nosed coach. You've got to get behind him to know what winning feels like, and he's going to have our back through it all. I'm just glad to

ABOVE: Andrej Stojakovic goes to the basket against Oregon. (Robin Scholz/The News-Gazette)
RIGHT: The Maryland defense cannot contain Andrej Stojakovic on a drive to the hoop. (Robin Scholz/The News-Gazette)

NOSKI
ESNEY
HELPING INJURED PEOPLE
Illinois
2
MILLS
7

be here. I think we all know what's at stake. The coaching staff is extremely passionate about what we have and what we could do later on in this tournament."

How Stojakovic handled that knee injury and another ankle injury that popped up in early February stood out to his teammates. So did the way he embraced expanding his game, leaving behind the need to always be the No. 1 option like he was a year earlier at Cal in lieu of maximizing his athleticism at both ends.

"He fights through adversity very well, whether that's him playing through adversity with a bad game or it's off-court adversity like injuries," Illinois forward Jake Davis said. "He has a strong willpower in his mind, and I think that's going to carry him a long way. It's great to see him where he is now — healthy and playing at the highest level he can.

"It's fun to see him really experience this. He's having a great time. He's not taking anything for granted and really loving it and living up to it. One of the main reasons I decided to come here was Illinois is in the tournament almost every year. I think that's one of the main reasons for him, too. He wanted to come to a school and compete at the highest level. I think Illinois provides that."

Stojakovic said he wouldn't change anything about his first season at Illinois, where he is averaging 13.3 points and is the top option off the bench now. Mostly because he's never been on a team quite like this one.

"A lot of these guys I'm going to be close with the rest of my life," he said. "A lot of players can't really say that in general. I'm just glad to be in this environment. Not everyone gets to play at this time of year. I'm an example of it. It took me three years to get here. I'm just very grateful to be a part of this team at this time."

Andrej Stojakovic is defended by Florida Gulf Coast guard Darren Williams. (Robin Scholz/The News-Gazette)

ILLINOIS
2

NCAA SECOND ROUND

ILLINI 76, VCU 55

March 21, 2026

Peaking at the right time

Illini dispatch VCU, head to Sweet 16 fresh and full of confidence

By SCOTT RICHEY
srichey@news-gazette.com

GREENVILLE, S.C. — Kylan Boswell untucked his jersey as he made his way off the court during the final minute of Saturday night's second-round NCAA tournament game against VCU, stopping what he was doing just long enough to pump up the crowd at Bon Secours Wellness Arena sitting behind the Illinois men's basketball team's bench.

Keaton Wagler repeated that gesture as he walked off the court behind his veteran teammate in the five-for-five line change substitution.

The actual celebration 67 seconds later was equally as composed. The reality of a game that had been decided for a while. Illinois didn't rush the court and dogpile at the logo after turning a tight first half into a 76-55 rout by the final buzzer in front of 14,178 fans.

Smiles were still etched on faces.

Hugs handed out from coaches to players.

Fans recognized for their support. Super soakers were unleashed on coach Brad Underwood in the locker room.

A win certainly worth celebrating, but also the expectation. Third-seeded Illinois (26-8) is chasing more and will get a shot at those loftier ambitions with a Sweet 16 showdown against second-seeded Houston (30-6) at the Toyota Center in Houston on Thursday night.

"I'm glad this year, with this team, we managed to get there," Illinois center Tomislav Ivisic said after watching his brother advance to the Sweet 16 with Arkansas last season, feeling like the Illini should have done the same.

"But nobody will satisfy themselves with that," Ivisic continued about reaching the Sweet 16. "We didn't come for that. We know what's waiting for us. I just feel the team is aware of the stakes now. We want to hang out a little bit more. We want to practice more. We want to play more games. We don't feel like it's our time to go home."

Illinois extended its season with a pair of dominant victories in South Carolina. The Illini crushed Penn 105-70 in the first round before fending off a first-half rally by VCU to run away with a 21-point victory on Saturday night.

The Rams (28-8) fell behind by double digits early in the first half before rallying to tie the game. A run Illinois expected after watching VCU do the same thing to North Carolina in the first round. The difference was the Illini had the answer the Tar Heels never discovered.

Andrej Stojakovic provided the momentum with his own personal 9-0 scoring run to end the first half and give Illinois a 35-28 halftime lead. Then Illinois' depth of offensive talent took center stage in the second half while the defense clamped down on the Rams.

"As much as we know what's at stake, we also understand we can't jump ahead," said Stojakovic, who scored a game-high 21 points. "We can't jump the gun. We knew VCU was going to come to the game extremely aggressive. We knew they weren't going to let up. They had a great comeback in the first round.

"Even when we were up big in the second half, we couldn't let our foot off the gas because we know that teams in March, that's what they're going to do. They were never going to let up because their season was at

David Mirkovic and Keaton Wagler celebrate their win over VCU. (Rob Le Cates/The News-Gazette)

Illinois

stake, just like ours was. Keeping that same mindset — keeping that aggression for 40 minutes — is what we've preached pretty much since we lost to Wisconsin."

That one-and-done experience in the Big Ten tournament stuck with Illinois. Probably because it wasn't the first time a big lead vanished and a winnable game turned into a crushing loss. Wisconsin did it in the regular season, too. So did Michigan State and UCLA.

Not letting VCU pull off a second come-from-behind upset — avoiding North Carolina's fate — was top of mind for the Illini.

"We wanted to make sure that wasn't us," Illinois forward Ben Humrichous said. Illinois outscored the Rams by 14 in the second half to secure the win.

"Some of the adversity that we faced through the year giving up big leads to end up losing was a big piece of what prepared us for these moments," Humrichous continued. "It's learning how to come together. Learning how bitter those moments tasted when you lose a game when you knew you should have won it. I think those moments prepared us."

Illinois had moments where it slipped against VCU. Missed shots and turnovers helped the Rams claw back from that initial first-half deficit. But the Illini never lost confidence. It's something they've held on to throughout the season.

Illinois center Tomislav Ivisic shoots over VCU forward Lazar Djokovic during the first half. (Associated Press)

"I would say that when we are mentally locked in — when everyone is dialed in and focused for 40 minutes over the course of the game — that we are pretty scary," Illinois forward David Mirkovic said. "We always believed and always thought we're the best team in the country. We've got to have that mindset. Even after the bad losses we had — the two Wisconsin losses, the UCLA loss — we always thought we had the best team. Now, we're just even better."

Better might be what it takes to knock off Houston on Thursday in the Sweet 16. Especially when you consider the Cougars will be playing so close to home. Like two miles between their own Fertitta Center and the Toyota Center where the next two rounds of the NCAA tournament will take place.

Houston crushed Texas A&M 88-57 in its own second-round blowout on Saturday. A 30-win team that now stands between Illinois and its ultimate goal. The Illini are still chasing that elusive national championship.

"It's why I came here," Underwood said. "It's why I'm still doing it. ... That's everything that drives me. The first day I feel like we can't win a national championship, they need to hire somebody else or I need to retire. We're in that mix."

David Mirkovic shoots the ball against VCU forward Michael Belle during the second half. (Associated Press)

8
High Point 81
Vanderbilt 102
Final
23
HOSTED BY
MARCH MADNESS

NCAA SWEET 16

ILLINI 65, HOUSTON 55

March 26, 2026

Not just another win

Domination of Houston — in Houston — shows the sky is the limit for this Illini team

By SCOTT RICHEY
srichey@news-gazette.com

HOUSTON — Watching Keaton Wagler dribble out the clock at the end of Thursday night's game against Houston generated a sense of disbelief for Andrej Stojakovic.

A surreal did-this-just-really-happen moment.

Then, the magnitude of Wagler standing near mid-court as the clock wound down at the Toyota Center struck.

It wasn't just another win for the Illinois men's basketball team in a season that's now included 27 of them to tie for the fourth-most in program history. It's late March. The stakes are infinitely higher.

It's why the celebration started before the final buzzer.

Zvonimir Ivisic bounced up and down, arms held high, facing the section of Illinois fans behind the team's bench. Assistant coaches Geoff Alexander and Orlando Antigua applauded.

As soon as the horn sounded, though, the celebration took on another level. Ben Humrichous hit as many chest bumps as possible. Kylan Boswell, too. Ivisic kept bouncing.

Because it wasn't just another win.

Illinois' 65-55 victory against Houston — in Houston, no less, in front of 17,307 fans — pushed its NCAA tournament run to the next level. An Elite Eight appearance at 5:09 p.m. Saturday against Big Ten rival Iowa that puts the Illini one win away from the Final Four.

"When you get off the court and see everybody cheering for you, the feeling is inexplainable," Stojakovic said. "We're so proud. We'll have these moments to cherish forever. I wouldn't change it for anything.

"We have faith in each other to make a deep run. We put so much work in. It's a great feeling to get to this point, but we understand that we've got a chance to do something that hasn't been done in a really long time for this program. We're excited about it."

That meant celebrating in the moment before the focus shifts to Saturday night's showdown with Iowa. As has become tradition, that includes a super soaker battle in the Illini locker room. The coaching staff, armed to the teeth, ambushed the players from an unexpected back door. Ty Rodgers popped out the front door to send several streams at the waiting media to, as he put it, include everyone in the celebration.

There was, of course, plenty to celebrate. Illinois (27-8) found itself in arguably the most challenging Sweet 16 matchup and never wavered. The Illini, in fact, provided Houston (30-7) the type of experience it typically lays on its opponents with a physical, 40-minute defensive effort that snuffed out the Cougars' biggest strengths.

"I think we just tried our best to make everything difficult," Boswell said. "I think our intensity and aggressiveness was maybe a little shocker for them because they're usually the ones who are doing that to others. We wanted to let them know, 'We're here, and nothing is going to be easy.'"

Neither team had it easy offensively in the first half where Illinois led 24-22 at the break. The Illini found their rhythm first and built an 18-point lead in the second half. A massive lead Illinois didn't squander this time

David Mirkovic battles with Houston forward Kalifa Sakho during the Illini's Sweet 16 win over the Cougars. (Moises Ramos Marin/The News-Gazette)

0

despite Houston cutting its deficit to single digits with just less than six minutes to play and again with less than two minutes on the clock.

Applicable lessons learned throughout the course of the regular season when similar leads fully disappeared proved fruitful on Thursday night. All against Big Ten opponents like Michigan State, UCLA and Wisconsin to name a few.

"How many times were we in that position — twice, three times — and we lost?" Humrichous said. "It was trying to remember some of those moments where we did relax and lost games. Really proud of our focus. I think everybody was confident and on the same page and ready to execute what we needed to do. It comes through your preparation, but it also comes through a season of adversity."

Boswell said the urgency of the situation kicked in for Illinois down the stretch. The regular-season games that saw commanding leads turn into disappointing losses always had a get-it-next-time feeling. That doesn't exist at this point in March.

"I think we're very focused," Illinois coach Brad Underwood said. "I think our mindset

RIGHT: Illinois center Tomislav Ivisic shoots between teammates Keaton Wagler (23) and Jake Davis against Houston. (Moises Ramos Marin/The News-Gazette)

FACING: David Mirkovic takes a shot over Houston guard Kingston Flemings. (Moises Ramos Marin/The News-Gazette)

Illinois
0

is in the right place. We know it's got to be 40 minutes. We've talked all year about the margins. We've talked all year about the little things. You can't take possessions off. You can't have bad moments. We had a few of those in the regular season. I give our guys a lot of credit.

"I've always said you want to throw the first punch. You don't want to take the chance of getting knocked out if they throw the first one and hit you. So, let's throw the first one. We took some blows, but I thought it was us who was in a good position to withstand them."

Withstood. Survived. Advanced.

Next up? A Big Ten rematch in the Elite Eight with a chance to keep chasing the ultimate goal.

"I think national championship every year," Underwood said. "That's what I talk about from the start. You've got to beat really good basketball teams to get there. You've got to have a little bit of luck on your side. It's a great opportunity. We've got a great opponent in Iowa. We'll have to play well."

David Mirkovic and Ben Humrichous react during the Sweet 16 win over Houston. (Moises Ramos Marin/The News-Gazette)

B1G
Illinois
3

NCAA ELITE 8
ILLINI 71, IOWA 59

March 28, 2026

'Better than I've ever dreamt'

Illini coach, players at a loss for words after overpowering Iowa for a trip to the Final Four

By **SCOTT RICHEY**
srichey@news-gazette.com

HOUSTON — Brad Underwood made his way up the ladder at the south end of the Toyota Center court with golden scissors in hand.

All it took were a few snips to finish the job his players and assistant coaches had started. Then what was left of the net was in Underwood's hand.

It was at that point the Illinois coach turned, arms raised, net draped around his neck, and pointed to the Illini fans in the stands. As much as the celebratory moment was for the Illinois team — players, coaches, managers, staff — Underwood made a point to acknowledge the support that made that moment possible.

A moment that will etch this Illinois team into program history after a 71-59 victory against Big Ten rival Iowa on Saturday night in Houston extended the Illini season.

Next stop: Final Four.

"It's better than I've ever dreamt it would be," Underwood said. "I knew we would get here. I don't mean that to sound arrogant. You know me, I'm not afraid, and I'm sure not going to run from a challenge. The greatest moment was standing on the ladder and holding the net because that was for the people.

"I could look up there and I could see the crowd. I could imagine what's going on on Green Street right now and on our campus. You come with a vision to try to make something great, and you understand you're creating memories for a lot of people. That's something I take a lot of enjoyment in. That's a really positive moment. I didn't doubt we would get there. I just didn't know when. I knew it was hard. I'm very, very grateful for everyone who helped along the way."

Saturday night's celebration took on many forms.

Offensive coordinator Tyler Underwood was the first to embrace his dad while Keaton Wagler again had the pleasure of dribbling out the clock for a second time in three days in Houston. A hug between father and son that turned into a group celebration with director of operations Joey Biggs and assistant coach Zach Hamer also wrapped up by the Illinois coach.

Zvonimir Ivisic got a Croatian flag from someone in the stands and immediately draped it across his shoulders. Tomislav Ivisic carried the Final Four trophy held high over his head. Kylan Boswell and Brandon Lee made off with a South Region bracket big enough that both were needed to carry it. Ben Humrichous shared a moment, alone, with his wife Adalia after celebrating with his team.

Celebration of a win Illinois knew was possible. Celebration of a spot in the Final Four Illinois knew it could claim.

"We know how good we are," Tomislav Ivisic said. "It's not even that. We know how hard we worked for these moments all summer listening to Coach Brad even when we don't want to. If somebody doesn't feel like practicing, you have to. That's your job. We pushed each other to do more for moments like this, and we're not done.

"We have a great, great team here. Great leadership from everybody. Everybody cares an insane amount. Everybody was dreaming of this moment. Nobody plays here for the

Keaton Wagler and Andrej Stojakovic chase the ball with Iowa's Kael Combs. (Moises Ramos Marin/The News-Gazette)

IOWA
11
Illinois
23
2
Wilson

name on the back, but the name on the front. Everybody got into their role and maybe took a little bit from themselves to give back to the team. That's what matters in the end. If you want to win as a team, that's what teams need to do. Sacrifice a lot for each other, play together and never give up."

The never give up part was necessary Saturday night against Iowa. The Hawkeyes scored the games first nine points and had a double-digit lead after just more than 4 minutes.

Illinois answered with a 9-0 run of its own immediately after Iowa pushed its lead to double figures. All of a sudden it was a ball game again. A close one, certainly, before the Illini began to pull away late in the second half and secured its 12-point victory with six consecutive made free throws between Wagler and Boswell.

"We expected them to be that aggressive," Illinois forward David Mirkovic said. "Our biggest point was to be locked in for 40 minutes. Just play for 40 minutes because basketball is a fast game, and it can turn in a second."

Mirkovic said he was fighting off tears in the final minutes of the game. Tracks ran down the face of associate head coach Orlando Antigua after shedding some a few tears of joy. And they were far from the only ones overcome by the emotions of this team reaching a Final Four — a first for Illinois in 21 years.

"I had so much adrenaline, so much emotion," said Mirkovic, adding Saturday's

Illini and Hawkeye players battle for a rebound beneath the basket. (Moises Ramos Marin/The News-Gazette)

SOUTH REGIONAL
#MARCHMADNESS
ELITE EIGHT
Illinois
Illinois
23
HOSTED BY

celebration was bigger than when SC Derby beat Partizan in the SuperCup. "I don't have the vocabulary to imagine this feeling. I forgot everything after the game finished. I don't remember anything. It was pure emotion.

"It's an unbelievable feeling. When a whole year you believe in something and after some bad games everyone doubts you and thinks you're not good, but you just know you're good and believe in each other. You've just got to wait — you've got to be patient — to prove all that. When that moment came, it's such a beautiful feeling, when you see all of your hard work paying off and all of your belief."

Zvonimir Ivisic said a few words wouldn't be enough to describe his feelings. That he would need a paragraph.

"We all believed," the 7-2 forward/center said. "We have a special group of guys who are willing to give everything — willing to sacrifice for each other — and it paid off. It means everything. Everything that we worked for. Everything that we dreamed of. We're one step closer to our goal."

That's the part Brad Underwood emphasized after the confetti had dropped, the nets were cut down and the super soakers emptied. Reaching the Final Four was just another step in the process.

"You can't just be happy to get there, and we're not going to do that," the Illinois coach said. "We're not wired that way. I'm not wired that way. We'll go compete."

RIGHT:: Brad Underwood and Tyler Underwood embrace after the win over Iowa. (Moises Ramos Marin/The News-Gazette)

FACING: Zvonimir Ivisic holds up his country's flag after an Elite 8 win over Iowa. (Moises Ramos Marin/The News-Gazette)

FINAL FOUR
IVISIC
2026 SOUTH
44
33
MEN'S

NCAA ELITE 8

ILLINI 71, IOWA 59

Final Four! Final Four!

By **BOB ASMUSSEN**
asmussen@news-gazette.com

HOUSTON — To quote the late, great Jim Turpin from 1989: Final Four! Final Four! Final Four!

For the first time since 2005, Illinois will be playing in the NCAA tournament semifinal. It wasn't easy.

Iowa built a 12-2 lead in the early going and stayed close deep into the game against favored No. 3 seed Illinois.

But a balanced offensive effort gave Illlinois a 71-59 victory.

And a trip late in the week to Indianapolis.

1. Keaton Wagler might have locked up his place in the Illinois Athletic Hall of Fame with an effort fans will be talking about for decades. The Big Ten's best freshman led Brad Underwood's team with 25 points Saturday night to lead Illinois back to the final four.

2. Already popular with the Illinois fan base, Tomislav Ivisic put himself on another level with his late-game heroics against Iowa. He finished with 13 clutch points before fouling out.

3. With his dad Peja back in the stands, Andrej Stokaovic was big off the bench with 17 points. Illinois wouldn't have made the Final Four without him.

Kylan Boswell slaps Illinois' name over the South Region line on the bracket. (Moises Ramos Marin/The News-Gazette)

4. Illinois built an 18-9 rebound advantage in the first half. At the TV timeout of the second half, the edge had grown to 12. David Mirkovic struggled on offense in the first half, hitting just 1 of 6 shots. But had seven rebounds. He finished with 12.

5. Give Purdue coach Matt Painter credit for a longer than usual pregame interview with TBS' Allie LaForce. He is trying to put the Boilermakers for the second time during his career. Painter is one of the best talkers among Big Ten coaches. He can fill up a notebook.

6. Last time Iowa made the Final Four, in 1980, Lute Olson was the coach. He went on to great success at Arizona, where he won an NCAA title in 1997 in a battle of the Wildcats.

7. That was annoying. With 7:43 left in the first half,the horn at the Toyota Center got stuck, blaring for 11 minutes. Kids (and adults) in the stands tried to plug their ears. Great chance for TBS to show commercials and make some cash. Iowa fans booed the sound system, according to Houston correspondent Dorothy Lillig.

8. Credit Underwood for another pleasant exchange with TBS sideline reporter Lauren Shehadi. He was positive about the ability of his team to rally. Illinois immediately went on a run to cut into Iowa's advantage.

9. News-Gazette legend Loren Tate has only covered Illinois in the Final Four twice for The News-Gazette. But he attended multiple Final Fours over the years thanks to longtime Illinois coach Lou Henson, who gave him his tickets. Tate remembers seeing Magic Johnson and Larry Bird play in the tournament. Very cool.

10. The one time Iowa reached the NCAA title game in 1956, Tate was there at Evanston. The great Bill Russell led San Francisco to a victory against the Hawkeyes.

The Illini team celebrates in front of fans after clinching a trip to the Final Four. (Moises Ramos Marin/The News-Gazette)

THE DAILY ILLINI
FINAL
FOUR
2026 NCAA MEN'S
FINAL
FOUR
INDIANAPOLIS
FINAL
FOUR
SOUTH REGIONAL CHAMPION

Illinois players celebrate with the South Regional trophy. (Moises Ramos Marin/The News-Gazette)

NCAA
MARCH MADNESS
SOUTH REGIONAL CHAMPION
FINAL FOUR
WE'RE NOT DONE
2026 SOUTH REGIONAL CHAMPS

Underwood thrives in dream job

By SCOTT RICHEY
srichey@news-gazette.com

INDIANAPOLIS — Brad Underwood made three trips from Macomb to Champaign during his decade as an assistant coach at Western Illinois.

None of those three games were particularly close. The Leathernecks, in all honesty, got rocked. In all three. Illinois victories all by an average of nearly 30 points.

That's what Chad Jones remembers most about the game he spent on the Western Illinois bench in Champaign as a Leathernecks assistant. Hard not to when one team so thoroughly handles the other.

"Honestly, the thing I remember most about the game is we got killed," Jones said. Lucas Johnson scored a team-high 15 points in a 76-53 Illinois victory on Nov. 19, 1999. "We didn't play particularly well."

But another moment from that game has popped in Jones' memory a couple times in the last decade. A conversation he had with Underwood on the bench during Western Illinois' shootaround where Jones' former coach turned coaching colleague told him for the first time that Illinois was his dream job.

"We were fortunate and got to play a lot of big places, and he never said that about anywhere else," Jones said. "I honestly didn't really think much about it. When you're at Western Illinois — and Western Illinois is the bottom of the barrel at the Division I level — you don't think that might actually happen."

Jones didn't have need to recall that moment until well later when Underwood was named the Illini's new coach in March 2017. Jones remembers the commentary at that time about why Underwood would leave Oklahoma State after just one season to take the Illinois job. He had the answer.

"Man, 20 years ago he said this was his dream job," Jones said. "It's just awesome to see."

The memory of that moment on the bench with Underwood at then-Assembly Hall resurfaced for Jones last weekend when Illinois clinched its first Final Four appearance in 21 years with a 71-59 victory against Iowa in Houston.

It's not quite the culmination of Underwood's nine seasons in Champaign. The Illini are still chasing a national championship this weekend in Indianapolis, with a Final Four showdown against Connecticut set for 5:09 p.m. Saturday. But cutting down the nets in Houston secured part of a dream.

Putting down roots

A dream that has roots in McPherson, Kan., and featured a path from Hardin-Simmons to Dodge City Community College, Western Illinois, Daytona Beach Community College, Kansas State, South Carolina, Stephen F. Austin and Oklahoma State before Underwood landed in Champaign.

"I've been blessed along the way because I've worked for nothing but winners for head coaches and people who allowed me to grow," Underwood said. "You work for Bob Huggins, you work for Frank Martin, you learn winning. They helped. I played for a legendary coach in Jack Hartman (at Kansas State). So, it's been maybe a different path than most, but there's not one step of it that I would give up because I've been beyond

Coach Brad Underwood is in the center of the Illini bench during a home game against Northwestern. (Robin Scholz/The News-Gazette)

KRAUS
ILLINOIS

blessed to work for great people who helped prepare me to get to these moments.

"I've never doubted us getting to a Final Four would happen. I have thought we have had other teams capable. But I also know how doggone hard it is to do it. For that, I just say thank you. I say thank you to everybody involved. I'm going to get emotional, but I've been doing this 39 years. You dream about this as a kid, and I dreamt about doing it at Illinois."

That dream was something those close to Underwood have known for decades.

The conversation the now Illinois coach had with Jones during their time at Western Illinois wasn't the only one he had while in Macomb.

Geoff Alexander heard the same thing.

Another former Leathernecks player turned assistant coach, Alexander followed Underwood from Western Illinois to what is now Daytona State College in Florida. They reconnected again after Underwood got the Illinois job, with Alexander landing in Champaign as assistant to the head coach before being promoted to assistant coach in 2021 and then additionally being named recruiting coordinator.

"At the time, Illinois was rolling," Alexander said. "They were a premier program. Being in the state for the 10 years he was at Western, on an everyday basis he was reminded what this program is about. This thing opens up, and there's not a better guy for this job. Nobody."

Landing Illinois job

Underwood coached his final game at Oklahoma State on March 17, 2017 — a 92-91 loss to Michigan in the first round of the NCAA tournament. The next day he was on a plane from Stillwater, Okla., to Champaign as Illinois' next coach. A move that started percolating earlier in the week after a phone call from Illinois athletic director Josh Whitman to Underwood's agent, Bret Just.

Just was in Dayton, Ohio, for the First Four when the Illinois job opened after Whitman fired John Groce. Just said he received a call from an unknown number with a 217 area code, and, against his typical practice, he answered.

"Josh and I had a quick chat," Just told The News-Gazette. "I tried to not show all my cards with my excitement level where I was kind of jumping through the windshield. I said, yeah, maybe there could be some interest.

"These things take on a life of their own. We did a really good job, I think, at the time, of keeping it under wraps. I think everybody was kind of shocked when it was announced, but it moved very, very fast."

Tyler Underwood played for his dad at Stephen F. Austin and Oklahoma State and remembers having the conversation about Illinois being a possible landing spot after the Cowboys returned home following their NCAA tournament exit that March.

It was exciting news for the Underwood family. Tyler Underwood was born in Macomb and the first basketball jersey he owned was, rather famously in Illinois circles, a Brian Cook Illini jersey.

"Knowing the passion that the fan base had, (Illinois) was a job he always thought was a really good one and a job he always followed," Tyler Underwood said about his

Brad Underwood works a referee during a win over Southern. (Robin Scholz/The News-Gazette)

dad. "I kind of maintained my Illinois fandom throughout my childhood as my dad was a JUCO coach.

"The job was very attractive. As a family, we always had the ultimate trust in my dad to make the right decision when it came to the job. Looking back now, I wouldn't change it for the world."

Just, like those others close to Underwood, knew how much his client-turned-friend valued the Illinois job. That's something Whitman learned when he met with Underwood and his family in Stillwater, Okla. It was in that moment in the Underwood's living room parallel tracks — the way Whitman and Underwood each viewed Illinois basketball — converged.

"I think we both knew what Illinois basketball was capable of," Whitman said. "Otherwise, I don't think either one of us would have wanted to be on that plane together. As the hours passed in his living room, we realized that he was somebody that I could trust that had a lot of the same values I had and had the same vision for what Fighting Illini basketball could become again. And I think, in me, he saw somebody he could trust to deliver on what this university is capable of and could be a good partner for him. It's better than I ever imagined, but really the culmination of a conversation we started nine years ago in Stillwater."

Growing pains early

Not that it was a quick fix for Underwood at Illinois after the program had slipped in the Big Ten — finishing eighth, seventh, 12th and ninth — and out of the NCAA tournament picture entirely during Groce's final four seasons as coach.

Underwood's first team went 14-18, tied for 11th in the Big Ten and missed the NCAA tournament.

Year two was worse.

Illinois set a program record for losses in a 12-21 season that featured a tie for 10th in the conference and a sixth straight season without an NCAA tournament appearance.

"Times were different then," Underwood said. "We didn't have the portal. We didn't have NIL where you could flip it quickly. The first two years were about establishing a culture. We couldn't get anybody to come. We missed out on everybody until Ayo (Dosunmu) jumped on."

The 62-year-old Underwood, who has made it clear patience is not his best trait during his time in Champaign, said Whitman had more than enough for the two of them. The fact his first two seasons in charge led to a record 13 games below .500 required that patience.

Two seasons that didn't sit well with a fan base hoping for a quick fix. Even with Underwood's eventual success, it still wasn't enough for some pockets of supposed Illinois supporters.

"When things weren't going well, I was telling people, 'You've just got to give the guy a chance,'" said Jones, now the Lincoln Land women's basketball coach. "I've always been a staunch defender of him from a distance. Talk about paying the price and waiting his turn, goodness gracious. He took the long road to get there, but he made it."

Whitman was steadfast in his support of Underwood. The Illinois athletic director knew the results wouldn't flip overnight, but

Brad Underwood congratulates his players after a win over Missouri in St. Louis. (Knox Mynatt/The News-Gazette)

SPORTS DRINK

he spent enough time embedded with the team — in practices, on plane rides, at games home and away — to see signs of progress.

"It was hard and it was tough and it was gritty and it was imperfect, but it was necessary," Whitman said. "Although we weren't seeing the results that any of us wanted on the court, I knew what was happening away from the court that was ultimately going to put us in position to be successful. I just never lost confidence in who he is and the leader he can be."

A different makeup

Underwood also never doubted Illinois could get back to this point. Get back to the Final Four. What he didn't lose, however, was the knowledge of how difficult that path can be. Something that was reinforced several times during his tenure in Champaign, including losing in the second round of the NCAA tournament as a No. 1 seed in 2021 and getting crushed by UConn in the Elite Eight in 2024.

Two talented teams. Two teams that couldn't stack the necessary six wins in late March and into April.

But reaching the Final Four — putting Illinois in position to win its first national title — has always been the dream. That, Alexander said, is what sets his boss apart.

"You may look at him like, 'Really?' and by golly he's going to fight, claw and do everything he can to knock out that dream," Alexander said. "That's just how he works. He's made up differently. It's always been that way. This isn't just (nine) years at Illinois. That's just his makeup and his DNA. This is something he has been fighting to get to his entire career.

"Every single day in the offices, a national championship is talked about. Every single day. He pounds, pounds messages into his staff and into his players, and it becomes reality."

All about relationships

The connective thread between Underwood's start at Hardin-Simmons to his decade at Western Illinois and every stop between Macomb and Champaign was the relationships he developed. That was the lens through which the Illinois coach discussed reaching the Final Four. How those relationships — those people in his life — were all part of his decades-long journey.

"It's never about Brad," Just said. "It's always about the people and his support network and his family and his former players and his staff and the (Western Illinois coach) Jim Kerwins of the world. If someone is going to spend 10 years as an assistant coach at Western Illinois, maybe they deserve an opportunity like this. It's the culmination of the relationships."

Like Underwood's relationship with Alexander.

It didn't take much convincing from Underwood to get his former assistant to join him in Champaign nine years ago. Their history meant no pitch was needed. Alexander knew Illinois and knew Underwood.

"I knew what was going to happen here when he took this job, and you're seeing it right now," Alexander said. "One of the things I told him the first time I talked to him after he took the Illinois job was, 'You can win it here,' and he said, 'You're damn right.'"

Brad Underwood is interviewed by the Big Ten Network following a win over Minnesota at the State Farm Center. (Robin Scholz/The News-Gazette)

BIG NETWORK

Kylan Boswell pauses to get a hug and a selfie with his grandma Judy Ford before boarding the bus to go to Indianapolis and the Final Four. (Robin Scholz/The News-Gazette)

David Mirkovic waves to fans as the Illini head to the court for practice at Lucas Oil Stadium before their Final Four matchup with Connecticut. (Robin Scholz/The News-Gazette)

Illinois guard AJ Redd is carried off court in celebration after winning the NCAA Elite Scholar-Athlete Award at Lucas Oil Stadium before the Final Four. (Robin Scholz/The News-Gazette)

Brad Underwood addresses his team during a public practice before the Final Four at Lucas Oil Stadium in Indianapolis. (Robin Scholz/The News-Gazette)

FIGHTING ILLINI
INDIANAPOLIS

Zvonimir Ivisic dunks while fans react on the video boards during a practice session before the Final Four. (Robin Scholz/The News-Gazette)

BONUS FLS TOL
0 4
10
3:17
1ST
TOL FLS BONUS
4
3:17

B1G
Illinois
23
15

Tipoff of the Illini's Final Four matchup with UConn at Lucas Oil Stadium in Indianapolis. (Associated Press)

FINAL FOUR
UCONN 71, ILLINI 62

April 4, 2026

Abrupt end hits hard

UConn plays a near-perfect game to bring Illini's dream season to a close

By SCOTT RICHEY
srichey@news-gazette.com

INDIANAPOLIS — The final seconds of Saturday's Final Four showdown between Illinois and Connecticut had yet to run off the clock, but reality had already hit.

David Mirkovic sat on the Illinois bench, towel held to his mouth and distant look in his eyes. Zvonimir Ivisic stood next to him with the towel draped around his neck gripped tightly in both hands.

There were still fouls to commit to stop the clock. Still free throws to shoot by the Huskies.

A perfunctory end to a game that looked like it might be another chapter in the lopsided Illinois-UConn series but had turned tense — close — in the final minutes after an Illini rally from a double-digit deficit.

A comeback that came up short. Playing from behind for nearly 25 minutes too much for Illinois to overcome in a 71-62 UConn victory.

The Illinois players filed off the court, down the tunnel and back toward their locker room after a quick handshake line. Heads bowed. Tears already starting to fall.

Tomislav Ivisic was the last off the court, but he wasn't alone. Ty Rodgers wrapped his arm around the 7-foot-1 center as the two walked down the steps from the raised court erected in the middle of cavernous Lucas Oil Stadium.

"I was trying to point to all the orange in the crowd, just showing him the support that he has behind him," Rodgers said. "I was telling him this won't be your last time here. I wasn't expecting him to say anything. That's how I would be after a loss as well.

"I wasn't doing it for a reaction out of him or anything. That's my brother. Just hearing those positive vibes is always good, and it's the truth. We got to the Final Four, and that's an accomplishment that most people don't get to experience."

Rodgers has spent the entire season on the Illinois bench after suffering a knee injury last June. That didn't lessen the impact he's had on this team and his teammates the last five-plus months. Saturday night wasn't any different.

"Even though he's not on the court, I always consider him our leader," Ivisic said. "He was here before all of us. He just wanted to let me know all these people were here for us, they were all extremely proud and to keep my head high."

That's how Illinois coach Brad Underwood wanted his team to treat Saturday's loss. That it happened can't be avoided. The disappointment can't be buried. But one loss didn't erase the litany of successes from November through March.

"I've said it in a positive way that this team had great, great joy for each other's successes," Underwood said. "It worked the other way (Saturday)."

Illinois found itself face to face with the potential end of its season after UConn turned an eight-point halftime lead into a double-digit advantage through the majority of the second half on the strength of more made three-pointers than the Huskies had managed during the rest of their tournament run.

Illinois rallied with Ivisic providing a spark for a 10-0 kill shot that cut its deficit to four.

Ty Rodgers puts his arm around Tomislav Ivisic as Illinois leaves the court for the final time this season. (Scott Ritchie/The News-Gazette)

SPALDING
13

But that's as close as the Illini got — with 5 minutes to play and again with 44 seconds on the clock — before UConn could finish off its Final Four victory.

"Coach Brad kept preaching trust and belief," Illinois forward Ben Humrichous said. "We walked in here at halftime down eight. We've been in that position before. This is a team that had second half runs because we trusted and believed all tournament long. It was trust and believe in the game plan we had that we all knew was proven successful. We just needed a few extra efforts in the first half, and that game would have looked different."

That trust and belief only got Illinois part of the way to a comeback. Not enough when the season has reached its win-or-go-home climax. The Illini, again, experienced the abruptness of the end only one team avoids each April.

"Nobody wanted the season to end," Illinois forward Jake Davis said was the fuel to the team's comeback attempt. "We all have fight in us. We all have that dog in us. We weren't going to give up. Nobody in this room was going to give up.

"This year hurts a little bit more because we got closer to the prize and fell short again. We accomplished something phenomenal, but it sucks to lose. It just sucks."

Illinois' season might have ended two days before the Illini wanted, but the bar was raised again for the program 21 years after its last Final Four appearance. It's the new standard in Champaign, Ivisic said, to make this kind run a regular occurrence.

For now, Illinois will absorb the sting of an NCAA tournament exit. Another team Underwood saw with the potential to win a national championship seeing its season end too soon.

"When they beat us in the Elite Eight, we were right there," Underwood said, referencing his team's loss to UConn in 2024. "That was a bad feeling. This is even worse. I thought we were a national championship caliber team. I'll say what I always say, and it sounds redundant, but I apologize, you just have to keep knocking on the door.

"Am I competitive? Does today stink? It hurts. My gut hurts so bad right now that I feel for all of them, but I'm also excited about the joy that we brought a lot of people in this run. We've got Illinois back to a level that they're in Final Fours again, and my God, as long as I'm the ball coach, I'd better not take 21 damned years to get back there."

ABOVE: Ben Humrichous blocks a Michigan dunk attempt during the Final Four. (Robin Scholz/The News-Gazette)

RIGHT: Andrej Stojakovic goes to the basket against the backdrop of Lucas Oil Stadium. (Robin Scholz/The News-Gazette)

SPALDING
ILLINOIS
FIGHTING ILLINI
UCONN
HUSKIES
ON THE COURT PTS REB AST STL BLK FLS
2 STOJAKOVIC 5 3 0 0 0 1
3 HUMRICHOUS 0 2 0 0 1 0
13 IVISIC 8 2 0 0 0 2
15 DAVIS 0 1 0 0 0 0
23 WAGLER 14 6 2 0 0 2
ON THE COURT PTS REB AST STL BLK FLS
1 BALL 6 0 1 0 0 0
2 DEMARY JR. 5 8 6 1 0 2
5 REED JR. 11 6 0 0 0 2
11 KARABAN 9 2 2 1 1 1
23 ROSS 6 1 0 0 0
FG 12/33 AST 2 BLK 4
2PT% 47 OREB 6 TO 5
3PT% 25 DREB 20 POT 0
FT% 73 STL 0 PITP 14
FG 16/42 AST 10
2PT% 37 OREB 6
3PT% 39 DREB 16
FT% 100 STL 3
BONUS FLS 4 TOL 3 36 14:41 2ND 49
CONNECTICUT
AND THEN THERE WERE

Bright future starts now

The focus for Underwood and Co. must shift ahead quickly after Final Four

By **SCOTT RICHEY**
srichey@news-gazette.com

INDIANAPOLIS — The college basketball world moves fast.

Faster still if a team has extended its season into the final weekend. Like Illinois, which will face just a two-day gap between a Final Four loss to Connecticut and the official start of the offseason when the transfer portal opens Tuesday.

That leaves little time for introspection on a 28-win season that ended two wins shy of a national championship. Work toward the 2026-27 roster — trying to piece together a group that could make another Final Four run — starts immediately.

Kylan Boswell, Ben Humrichous and AJ Redd are the only players on the Illinois roster who exhausted their eligibility Saturday night against the Huskies. Everyone else could return. How many actually will is the question.

Will Keaton Wagler parlay his breakout freshman season into his expected lottery pick status in the 2026 NBA Draft? Can Illinois retain core members of its rotation? Who might be on the radar to fill what roster spots may open beyond incoming freshmen Lucas Morillo, Quentin Coleman, Ethan Brown and Landon Davis?

All legitimate questions. Zero with firm answers in the aftermath of Saturday's season-ending loss in Indianapolis.

"Honestly, right now I haven't really thought of that," Wagler said about his future. "I couldn't really answer that question right now."

Answers from Wagler's teammates with their own stay-or-go decision to make weren't, collectively, all that much clearer. But, in this era of college basketball, the question had to be asked.

"I don't know," Tomislav Ivisic said. "The game just ended, and there's a lot to think about. I've always enjoyed being here, so we'll see what comes next."

Ty Rodgers and Jake Davis, at least, seem intent on another year in Champaign. Rodgers said he expects to get a medical redshirt after missing the entire 2025-26 season following offseason knee surgery.

"Obviously, there will be some coaches meetings like there always is, but as of right now I'm I-L-L," the veteran Illinois wing said.

"I love Illinois," Davis added. "I don't intend on leaving. Obviously, things change, but I haven't really thought about it to this point. I was worried about winning a national championship. But I love Illinois."

Andrej Stojakovic adeptly side-stepped a question about his future. But the Illinois guard understands what could be possible in 2026-27 in Champaign.

"We've all got decision to make," Stojakovic said. "We understand certain guys could come back and we could do something really special. Obviously, everybody has to go talk to their family and make the smartest decision for themselves, but this program, clearly the most fun I've had out of the three programs I've been to. The memories we have — the personalities we had on this team — you can't take that away from us. I'm glad we had this year."

Brad Underwood's message for his players that could return next season was simple: "Please come back. Let's go do this again."

Brad Underwood looks on alongside his son, assistant coach Tyler Underwood, late in a Final Four loss to Michigan. (Robin Scholz/The News-Gazette)

What Underwood didn't anticipate being a challenge is selling other players on Illinois this offseason. Not after a 28-win season that included a Final Four appearance.

The door won't be wide open, though.

"We're still going to be selective," the Illinois coach said. "We're not for everybody. We're really not. We're going to find the guys that want to be in that locker and want to play the right way. We're not for everybody, but it's sure a good selling point.

"You've got to go find those guys, and you can win. The talent pool is not huge at the highest level, but you've got to find guys you can coach and find guys that want to play the right way."

Whatever the situation — however many players Illinois is able to retain or add — Underwood is confident in his staff's ability to piece together another roster that works. A roster that fits.

"We can work on Xs and Os and all that, but meshing personalities and people is why our staff is so good," Underwood said. "Sometimes it takes a little time and there's a loss or two in there, but when you've got a staff who works as hard as you do and every single one of them's in tears, they're invested and they're invested for the right things. We'll be back."

• • •

The 72,111 fans who filled Lucas Oil Stadium on Saturday night for a pair of Final Four games included an impressive number in orange. That support wasn't lost on the Illinois players or their coach.

Even after the loss to UConn.

"The way the fans love us and the way that we love them, it didn't feel like we lost," Stojakovic said. "Honestly. You understand the game's over and you lost, but how loud it was and the way they looked at you, clapping at you, yelling for you, it's truly special how many people came out to support us."

The message Wagler said he heard the most from the fans as he walked off the court was for the Illini to keep their heads up.

"Getting to the Final Four hadn't happen in over 20 years," Wagler continued. "Them continuously showing us support makes us feel good about it even though we didn't get the outcome we wanted."

Illinois fans didn't just show up Saturday night in Indianapolis. They made the trips to Greenville, S.C., and Houston. They flooded Willard Airport after the team returned following its Elite Eight victory against Iowa. They crammed the team's hotel lobby before Saturday's game.

"You can't ask for anything better, any more support," Underwood said. "They fell in love with the team. They've treated me great. Now that we've lost I hope that stays the same, but, wow, did they show up.

"I hope this team is remembered, and I hope along the way that everybody who was here has at least somewhat of a good memory. The outcome of the game was disappointing, but I hope they had a great time. We've got the best fans in the country. I'll go to my death bed believing that."

Keaton Wegler leads the Illini onto the court ahead of their Final Four matchup against UConn. (Robin Scholz/The News-Gazette)

Illinois
23
B1G
IT IN.

The 2025-26 Illinois Fighting Illini.
(Robin Scholz/The News-Gazette)

ILLINOIS
44
ILLINOIS
31
ILLINOIS
0
ILLINOIS
23
ILLINOIS
15
ILLINOIS
77
ILLINOIS
4

DATE	OPPONENT	RESULT	W-L (CONF)	High Points	High Rebounds	High Assists
Mon, Nov 3	vs Jackson State	W113-55	1-0 (0-0)	Humrichous 21	Mirkovic 14	Boswell 5
Fri, Nov 7	vs Florida Gulf Coast	W113-70	2-0 (0-0)	Boswell 31	Mirkovic 11	Boswell 3
Tue, Nov 11	vs Texas Tech11	W81-77	3-0 (0-0)	Stojakovic 23	Ivisic 7	Boswell 3
Fri, Nov 14	vs Colgate	W84-65	4-0 (0-0)	Mirkovic 27	Mirkovic 21	Boswell 4
Wed, Nov 19	vs Alabama	*L90-86	4-1 (0-0)	Stojakovic 26	Mirkovic 10	Boswell 7
Sat, Nov 22	vs Long Island University	W98-58	5-1 (0-0)	Stojakovic 20	Mirkovic 8	Wagler 3
Mon, Nov 24	vs UT Rio Grande Valley	W87-73	6-1 (0-0)	Stojakovic 24	Wagler 8	Mirkovic 5
Fri, Nov 28	vs UConn	*L74-61	6-2 (0-0)	Boswell 25	Ivisic 10	Boswell 3
Sat, Dec 6	vs Tennessee	*W75-62	7-2 (0-0)	Wagler 16	Wagler 8	Wagler 5
Tue, Dec 9	@ Ohio State	W88-80	8-2 (1-0)	Wagler 23	Mirkovic 9	Wagler 5
Sat, Dec 13	vs Nebraska	L83-80	8-3 (1-1)	Boswell 20	Stojakovic 10	Wagler 10
Mon, Dec 22	vs Missouri	*W91-48	9-3 (1-1)	Wagler 22	Ivisic 11	Mirkovic 5
Mon, Dec 29	vs Southern	W90-55	10-3 (1-1)	Davis 15	Wagler 7	Wagler 10
Sat, Jan 3	@ Penn State	W73-65	11-3 (2-1)	Boswell 18	Mirkovic 10	Wagler 3
Thu, Jan 8	vs Rutgers	W81-55	12-3 (3-1)	Wagler 17	Stojakovic 8	Boswell 5
Sun, Jan 11	@ Iowa19	W75-69	13-3 (4-1)	Wagler 19	Mirkovic 12	Mirkovic 5
Wed, Jan 14	@ Northwestern	W79-68	14-3 (5-1)	Wagler 22	Ivisic 7	Boswell 6
Sat, Jan 17	vs Minnesota	W77-67	15-3 (6-1)	Ivisic 18	Ivisic 9	Wagler 5
Wed, Jan 21	vs Maryland	W89-70	16-3 (7-1)	Stojakovic 30	Stojakovic 9	Wagler 8
Sat, Jan 24	@ Purdue4	W88-82	17-3 (8-1)	Wagler 46	Mirkovic 8	Wagler
Thu, Jan 29	vs Washington	W75-66	18-3 (9-1)	Wagler 22	Mirkovic 6	Wagler 8
Sun, Feb 1	@ Nebraska5	W78-69	19-3 (10-1)	Wagler 28	Ivisic 8	Wagler 5
Wed, Feb 4	vs Northwestern	W84-44	20-3 (11-1)	Stojakovic 17	Ivisic 12	Wagler 5
Sat, Feb 7	@ Michigan State	L85-82 OT	20-4 (11-2)	Mirkovic 18	Ivisic 8	Mirkovic 6
Tue, Feb 10	vs Wisconsin	L92-90 OT	20-5 (11-3)	Wagler 34	Ivisic 11	Wagler 7
Sun, Feb 15	vs Indiana	W71-51	21-5 (12-3)	Mirkovic 25	Humrichous 8	Mirkovic 3
Wed, Feb 18	@ USC	W101-65	22-5 (13-3)	Stojakovic 22	Davis 7	Boswell 8
Sat, Feb 21	@ UCLA	L95-94 OT	22-6 (13-4)	Wagler 19	Wagler 8	Wagler 6
Fri, Feb 27	vs Michigan	L84-70	22-7 (13-5)	Wagler 23	Mirkovic 10	Wagler 3
Tue, Mar 3	vs Oregon	W80-54	23-7 (14-5)	Stojakovic 21	Stojakovic 12	Wagler 5
Sun, Mar 8	@ Maryland	W78-72	24-7 (15-5)	Mirkovic 22	Mirkovic 11	Mirkovic 3
BIG TEN TOURNAMENT						
Fri, Mar 13	vs Wisconsin	*L91-88 OT	24-8 (15-5)	Mirkovic 19	Stojakovic 7	Wagler 8*
NCAA FIRST ROUND						
Thu, Mar 19	vs Pennsylvania	*W105-70	25-8 (15-5)	Mirkovic 29	Mirkovic 17	Wagler 7
NCAA SECOND ROUND						
Sat, Mar 21	vs VCU	*W76-55	26-8 (15-5)	Stojakovic 21	Ivisic 11	Mirkovic 4
NCAA SWEET 16						
Thu, Mar 26	vs Houston	*W65-55	27-8 (15-5)	Mirkovic 14	Wagler 12	Wagler 3
NCAA ELITE 8						
Sat, Mar 28	vs Iowa	*W71-59	28-8 (15-5)	Wagler 25	Mirkovic 12	Wagler 3
NCAA FINAL FOUR						
Sat, Apr 4	vs UConn	*L 71-62	28-9 (15-5)	Wagler 20	Wagler 8	Wagler 2

** Neutral site*

HARRISON 1996-08
7 35
QTR
49
TOL FLS BONUS
3 5
2026 NCAA
FOUR